# A GA

# MENTORING

Planting Your Life in
Another and Releasing the
Fragrance of Christ

Esther Burroughs

New Hope
Birmingham, Alabama

If you would like to have Esther Burroughs speak to your church, ministry, or organization, please contact:

Esther Burroughs Ministries
(864) 242-9624
Fax: (864) 242-9898
Email: melodyreid@aol.com


New Hope Publishers
P. O. Box 12065
Birmingham, Alabama 35202-2065
www.newhopepubl.com

Dewey Decimal Classification: 248.843
Subject Headings: CHRISTIAN LIFE—WOMEN
                  MENTORS
                  WOMEN—RELIGIOUS LIFE

Scripture quotations indicated by NASB are from the NEW AMERICAN STANDARD BIBLE ®, © Copyright The Lockman Foundation 1960, 1962, 1963, 1968, 1971, 1972, 1973, 1975, 1977. Used by permission.
       Scripture quotations indicated by NIV are from the Holy Bible, New International Version. Copyright © 1973, 1978, 1984 International Bible Society. Used by permission of Zondervan Bible Publishers.
       Scripture quotations indicated by *The Message* are from *The Message*. Copyright © 1993, 1994, 1995. Used by permission of NavPress Publishing Group.

Cover design by Steve Diggs & Friends
Back cover photo by Favorite Studios/Jacksonville, Florida

Illustrations by Amy Giles

ISBN: 1-56309-197-6
N974101•0499•5M3

# Dedicated to Jo Vaughn

What a great opportunity for me to tell you what your walk with the Lord has done for me. You have been a mainstay in my own walk with the Father—a support—an encourager. You have prayed, cried, and laughed with me for over 30 years. Not many people can claim a love and friendship like that. I know this is possible only through God. Ours is a friendship blessed by God. Your relationship and journey with God have been a beacon in my life. Your faith has been steady, constant, unwavering, and on target for me to observe and desire for my own life. *Faith* and *friendship* are words that to me best describe your mentoring me.

Yes, Jo, I did choose to put your words in this book because what you said to me, in describing me as one of your mentors, is exactly how I feel about your mentoring in my life. So I choose to say back to you your words in this dedication.

*Esther Burroughs*

 *Contents*

# Foreword

*The Secret Garden* by Frances Hodgson Burnett, a well-loved literary classic, is all the title implies. It is a mystery, but it is also a passionate and fervent love story. It is a story about the love of nature and of isolated human beings—human beings who learn to care for others and for themselves.

The primary character in *The Secret Garden* is *Mary Lennox*—a ten-year-old orphan, whose parents died in India during a plague. Mary was raised by a raja and is a very spoiled child who cares only about herself. She is sent to England to live with her uncle, *Archibald Craven*, in Misselthwaite Manor.

One night Mary discovers *Colin Craven*, the ten-year-old son of Archibald, hidden away in a remote wing of the manor. Ill, bedridden, anticipating the crippling distortion of his frail body by a hunchback which has not yet materialized, and fearing an early death, he is equally spoiled. Colin rules his servants like a young raja, throws temper tantrums when he is vexed, and allows no one to see him but a few personal servants, his doctor, and his father.

*Dickon Sowerby* is the 12-year-old brother of *Martha,* who is one of Mary's servants. Dickon is a Yorkshire lad who, as Mary comes to realize, is not like anyone else in the world. He can charm foxes, squirrels, and birds just as some people in India can charm snakes and . . . he is nicer than any other boy that has ever lived. He's like an angel.

For me, a very important character in the book is *Susan,* Dickon and Martha Sowerby's mother. A mother of 12 children, she is rich in her poverty. Her life is full of love as she empowers her children to take responsibility, love the earth, and live in grace with others. Mrs. Sowerby could have been a modern woman because she works inside and outside her home. She is full of earthy wisdom, cheer, and grace. Her garden is a lifeline for the nurture of her soul, her family, and others.

The garden itself is central to the story. Once loved and cared for, it comes into ruin after the death of Mrs. Craven. The garden is closed, the key to the door thrown away, and the beauty forgotten. Forgotten, that is, until Mary comes to live in the manor. She discovers the garden as the garden discovers her. Mary meets Dickon, and her life changes through his friendship to her and the garden. As Mary and Dickon nurture the garden, Mary herself is nurtured and she begins to nurture Colin. Colin chooses then to live, ultimately causing his father to begin to live and love again.

As the garden's beauty is rediscovered, so is life at Misselthwaite Manor. This is a story of *grace upon grace*, as one life is poured into another life—*empowered living*—impacting the world.

What a profound effect one person can have on the world, by investing in another's life. The choice to mentor can impact a life, a community, and ultimately, the Kingdom of God.

When I consented to write this book, I was immediately reminded of the many godly women and men who have planted in the garden of my life, calling me to accountability for my gifts in the Kingdom of God. I am bits and pieces of many. Each person showed me their love story with God. Each person drew me into the fragrance of God in their lives, showing me the garden path of fragrance that 2 Corinthians 2:14–15 (*The Message*) describes: *"In the Messiah, in Christ, God leads us from place to place in one perpetual victory parade. Through us, he brings knowledge of Christ. Everywhere we go, people breathe in the exquisite fragrance. Because of Christ, we give off a sweet scent rising to God, which is recognized by those on the way of salvation."*

# Introduction

I watched as she marked off the boundaries. It was as if she had a *Better Homes and Gardens* picture in her head and it took shape as she worked the soil. Daily, I could see the changes in the yard as she removed the sod, added bedding soil and mulch, and made room for the garden she had planned in her heart. It seemed every time I passed her yard, she was on her knees working in the soil. I've seen her swipe her forehead with earth-covered hands, leaving dirt smudges on her face—but that never covered the joy in her heart. As her neighbor, I am the recipient of the beauty that surrounds her home and now enhances mine.

Seeing my neighbor work so diligently in her garden awakened in me the desire to plan and plant my own garden. My neighbor became my wise advisor and coach. She knows so much more about gardening than I ever had the opportunity to learn, and now, her garden knowledge is helping me.

## Human Gardens

Creating a garden in the life of another woman is very much like planting and nurturing a beautiful flower garden. The boundaries must be set and the garden planned for just the right amount of exposure to the Son. The soil of her life must be worked, removing some things and adding others. The gardener will work hard and will need to spend a lot of time on her knees.

The gardener in this book is the godly woman who mentors; the garden is her mentee, the person in whom she chooses to plant her life. In each chapter you will find discussion of some aspect of gardening and related mentoring issues, followed by stories to illustrate the point and a summary of mentoring tips, or garden keys to mentoring, which are marked by this icon.

Christian women must be challenged to plant seeds in the lives of other women—to mentor, trusting their God-given spiritual gifts, natural talents and, perhaps, some hidden abilities;

using the proper tools; working intentionally; and trusting that the seeds, showered with the Sonlight of Christ, will produce a beautiful and fragrant garden.

## Who Can Mentor?

Some of the best modeling and mentoring may take place in the family. Bobb Biehl says, "Mentoring is the relational glue that can hold our generation to the last and to the next."

If, as parents, we don't mentor our children, who will? Parents must be involved in mentoring. However, when parents fail to do so or when parents aren't enough—and even when parents are enough—there are others who can and should be mentoring.

Gigi Tchividjian Graham recalls:

> I remember spending the night at my grandparents'
> home. Waking in the upstairs sleeping porch, I would just
> lie there for a moment, savoring the fragrance drifting
> upstairs. When I reached the bottom landing, I would
> peer around the corner into the living room. And my
> grandfather . . . would be there, just as he was every
> morning of his life—on his knees in front of the big red
> rocking chair. I knew this active surgeon, church layman,
> writer, former missionary to China, and family man had
> been up long before dawn, spending time with the Lord.
> He had an extensive prayer list, and I felt warm and
> secure, knowing he had already prayed for me. You
> don't learn compassion from a book or lecture. You learn
> it by experience and example.

Recently, a national newsmagazine hailed grandparents as *the silent saviors*. Psalm 127:3 tells us children are a gift from the Lord. I believe parents and grandparents can be used of God in sharing our walk with God, sharing our prayer life, and passing on to succeeding generations our spiritual heritage.

Not long ago, our first grandchild, Anna, started first grade. Bop (that's what our three granddaughters call my husband, Bob) and I sent a small bouquet of daisies—with a note of blessing to Anna, and the promise of Psalm 32:8. We called her the night before that first day of school, and prayed with her over the phone. She softly thanked us. Her mother called back, tearfully thanking us for our involvement in Anna's life. I have spent much time on the phone with my daughter talking through feelings and problems. I've spent a lot of time on my knees with my Father in mentoring prayer. What higher call and privilege is there than for parents and grandparents to impact families through prayer.

In today's world, the best models for many are not their fathers and mothers, but their teachers, coaches, and other outside influences. There is a real need for the church family to choose to become involved in what has become known as *spiritual parenting*. Parents in this culture, living a distance from their immediate families, need this spiritual parenting. The Church has so much to share, to model, and to use in mentoring.

We are in desperate need of mature women—I mean mature mentally and spiritually, not physically—who are willing to show God at work in their lives. Age is not the determining factor.

I have a friend named Beth whose longtime walk with God has been tested in the fires of hurt—a wayward daughter, a son struggling to find work, another daughter with a mentally handicapped child, and a mother with Alzheimer's disease. Her strength through these crises and her approachable manner have marked her as a woman to call for compassionate counsel. Many women consider Beth their mentor.

Don't let age be an issue. Let *life's lessons* be the qualifier. Mature women will cultivate love in another woman's life because of the King's presence in her life.

Lowe's advertisements in *Southern Living* magazine are so well done, and often have great truths embedded in the content. This is one such advertisement: "She's only five, but she wants to help mommy with her garden. So you show her how to push the seeds into the soil with her tiny fingers and how to water them just enough so they'll flourish. Then, when the first sprouts appear, you can see her amazement at what she's accomplished. This year, instead of a garden, you've cultivated a gardener."

Isn't that an amazing thought—cultivating *gardeners*, instead of gardens. Anyone can mentor! Age is not nearly as important as what you have to give. Mentoring, in many ways, means using the best part of yourself to help another see and become the best that they can be. Using what you know and what you have experienced, draw up alongside another woman and work side-by-side with her, teaching her and guiding her as you go. You, too, could be cultivating a gardener by mentoring!

## The Need Is Great

The note was simple: "Who would have known three years ago, when I invited you to participate in this conference, I would be in such need of healing, and that God would use you to begin that healing in me."

That kind of encouragement exemplifies the need for mentoring today. The woman speaking those words has served as a mentor to many women in her local church. And yet, as she honestly shared, she was hurting and needed a mentor herself.

Little did she know that the person who mentored her was also speaking out of deep hurt and unanswered questions in her own life! Isn't God good—in allowing us to mentor through our own pain and joy and without having all the questions answered? When we are vulnerable in mentoring, the mentee sees a real person working through life. Vulnerability becomes a source of great hope.

I don't know anyone in life who has not known hurt of some kind. Perhaps that is the qualifier in having something to say or having earned the right to be a mentor and to be heard. It is as the Master Gardener works in the soil of our lives—planting, feeding, pruning, and grooming—that we are empowered to share the fragrance with others. As the Master Gardener works in our hearts, our lives actually change. This change enables us to lead and empower others to follow the garden path, releasing the fragrance of Christ in their own lives.

So many needs! So many gardens waiting to be tended!

## Bouquets of Thankfulness

An Easter season spent in Richmond, Virginia, holds treasured memories for me and Bob. In the sitting room of the bed-and-breakfast where we stayed, I discovered a little book called *The Language of Flowers*. It was a very old book, so I gently looked inside, and discovered the author had given the names and meanings of flowers from A to Z. On each page, beautiful flowers were wonderfully illustrated in watercolor. I felt as if I were holding a very special gift.

I was mesmerized with the discovery that flowers had definitions. I wished for this treasure to be my own. I asked the innkeeper where I could find the book. She made several phone calls, but to no avail. As we pulled away from the inn and headed downtown for lunch, I had given up on ever finding it.

The place we chose to eat lunch, much to my delight, was surrounded with boutiques. After lunch, we entered a little shop that was really three shops in one, and one part contained antiques. Of course, I found several things our granddaughters just had to have, but Bob suggested we visit other shops before making a purchase—just like a man.

As he was leaving the store, I heard him say, rather excitedly, "Esther, you are not going to believe this!" He was pointing to the store window.

There in the antique shop window was *The Language of Flowers*—the very same book! I ran back inside, went to the window, picked up the book, looked for the price and found the letters NFS—not for sale. The shop owner found the owner of the book, who agreed to meet after lunch.

What a delight it was to finally meet Martha, a very elegant Virginia woman. Of course, I told her the whole story of finding the book at the inn and of writing this book about garden mentoring. I told her about my idea for using the flower names as a model—to show how we present bouquets to each other and to the Father. She listened intently and then said, "Then of course, you must have this book!" I was thrilled and elated!

The author said that Rose Musk Cluster means *charming*—and that is exactly the bouquet Martha gave to me that day in her shop. Thank you, Martha.

This unusual dictionary of the traditional meanings of more than 700 flowers is reminiscent of a gentler era when people found time to express their affection in an individual way. Scattered throughout this book, you will find bouquets of thankfulness from me to those who have mentored me, guiding me along the path perfumed with the fragrance of Christ. I pray that you, too, will give bouquets of thankfulness to those who have mentored you, and that some day you will receive bouquets of thankfulness from those you have mentored.

# Part One
# Principles *of* Garden Design

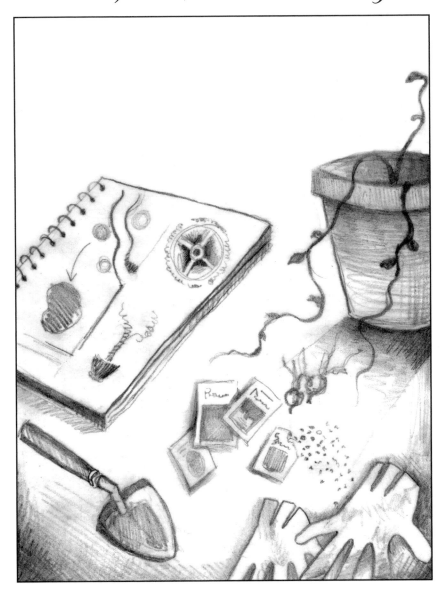

# I

## *This Is It!*

You will invest a great deal of time and effort in your garden.
Therefore, the importance of carefully selecting a site cannot be
stressed enough. A well placed garden yields hours of pleasure;
a poorly placed garden gives back endless frustration and produces regrets over wasted time and effort.

### Selecting a Site

Choosing my own garden location was not difficult because my
yard is quite small. I desired two things of my garden dream:
one, I wished to be able to sit on a bench in my informal English garden and see our small lake from the best vantage point;
and two, I wanted to be able to see the beauty of the garden
from my kitchen window.

Even when my garden plans were still on paper, I had already
raised the shutters and opened the window space to view where
my garden would be. It was on paper and in my imagination
long before a single seed went into the ground. Is that planning
or what?

One of the questions you must ask yourself if you are serious
about mentoring is: *Who will I mentor?* Just as I lifted my shutters
to view the spot where my garden would be, you will need to
keep your ears and eyes open and be looking for those persons
who need a mentor.

Begin with prayer. Think about the women you already know
in your church, the school system, your office complex, or in
your neighborhood. You should be careful to take your time in
choosing a woman to mentor. Ask God to show you a woman
who needs a mentor. Ask God to open your eyes to see the possibilities. Consider praying with a friend about the possibility of
mentoring someone, and perhaps, both of you will become
mentors in the process.

If a woman approaches you, asking you to mentor her, tell

her that you will need to think and pray about it. Don't be hasty in saying *yes* or *no*. Pray over this decision and think about all the possibilities just as if you were looking for a mentee.

Look with a loving heart to women in your church or neighborhood. Imagine the difference you could make in their lives as a mentor. Where will you plant yourself? Envision the garden possibilities. Raise the shutters and take a look around you.

## Be Intentional

When I decided to plant a garden, I was intentional about selecting where my garden would go. I thought through the possibilities and picked the best spot.

In preparation for the writing of this book, I sent out letters asking leaders about mentoring and the mentors in their lives. One of the questions I asked was, "When did you become a mentor?" I was very surprised that 95 percent said they were not aware until *after the fact* that they had been mentors. Many said, "I found myself doing what my mentors had done with me."

In this generation, we must not take the chance of learning about mentoring after the fact. We must intentionally and prayerfully seek out mentees.

Recently I read in *Leadership Net Fax* that there are four things that the Generation X group is asking from the church: love me, show me, guide me, and work beside me. What an invitation to change the world!

This is the first generation of divorce and perhaps divorce again. They lack family stories, traditions, and histories. For example, I know that my grandfather helped start the school and built the road in the community that he homesteaded. I have great stories of growing up with family—grandparents, aunts and uncles, cousins—and a community that helped parent me.

Generation X may not know these things about their family. Look what I have to pass down to this new generation who wants to connect with me. I could help them start family traditions—rituals that will change their family and hopefully pass on through their children to the next generation.

Look for women 5 to 12 years younger than you. They are out there—and they need you! Look for a woman in whose life soil you can nurture both life and gifts.

Years ago, I remember hearing one of my mentors speak to young women, and I thought, *I want to be like that when I grow up.* In retrospect, it wasn't that I wanted to be like that person so much as I wanted to know God and be able to tell about it like she did. Every time I heard she was speaking, I would go to hear her. I watched. I observed. I listened. I learned about her walk with God. I received from her valuable help with my parenting skills. I saw the world through her missions heart.

I would never have thought about asking someone like her how she got started speaking; and yet today, I often have young women ask me how they can become a speaker. How wonderful that they have the freedom to ask. How wonderful to be able to share my story—giving them encouragement and giving God all the credit. Think how much more I would have learned if I'd had the courage to ask my mentor, Marge Caldwell, to spend time with me. Think of it. If God can—and He did—take a shy, young Canadian girl, gift her as an athlete, and through her secondary education degree, allow her to speak throughout the United States and around the world, imagine what He can do with you and your gifts!

As I was writing this chapter, Marge called me—just, as she said, "to hear my voice and check on me." Thank you, Marge! Locust trees, *elegance*

Many years after hearing Marge Caldwell speak that first time, I have had the delightful privilege of working closely with her in women's meetings, and she is still my role model and mentor. I've kept every love note she has ever written to me through the years. I know God better because I know Marge better.

Be intentional in selecting someone to mentor (or, in finding someone to mentor you). If you notice a shy, young woman who hangs on your every word, pray about the possibility of mentoring her. It may be just what she needs, but is too shy to ask for. On the other hand, don't take on the task of mentoring every bold, young woman who asks you to do so. In each instance, prayer and careful consideration of what you might or might not have to offer are important. Intentionality implies purpose, design, and a long-range view of the possibilities, not random or impulsive selection.

## Knowing the Season

Winter contains spring. Spring gives way to summer. Summer calls for autumn, and autumn rests in winter.

Life is ordered by seasons. Gardens have seasons and follow a natural order. Perhaps we might describe the seasons of life in this manner:

- spring—birth; new life springing up
- summer—rapid growth; reaching toward the sun
- autumn—flowering; harvesting; the peak of color
- winter—maturing; dying back so that new growth may appear in the spring that follows

On the surface, this seems to be the natural order of things—each season with a specific purpose. New life appears in spring, grows throughout the summer, reaches its peak in the fall, and then dies in the winter.

It seems only natural to assume that someone in the winter or fall of her life should be nurturing, or mentoring, someone in the spring or summer of her life. The old mentor the young. It is natural. Older women have so much to offer younger women—experience, knowledge, and wisdom that come only from having been there and then slowing down to review.

And yet, even in nature, there are exceptions to what seems to be the natural order, like bulbs that blossom in the winter or early spring and then die back in the summer.

Season of life, or age, alone cannot define a mentoring experience. The desire and the need to mentor or be mentored may come at any season in life. The young and particularly mature woman may be able to mentor the older and less mature woman in some instances. A woman in the winter of her life may need the mentoring of another woman her age. The young may experience periods of quick growth only to go through many dying back phases. A woman may reach midlife only to discover a time of new life and learning.

A woman's experience and maturity, not her age, define her ability to mentor.

## The Importance of Women Mentoring Women

In today's culture, we must recognize the many separations in families—usually centering around the three *D's:* dysfunctional, distance, divorce. Never before has there been a time in the history of mankind when cross-generational nurturing is more needed in our society. We no longer have the luxury of being

## Definitions of Mentoring

- *Mentoring*—sharing the seeds of God's impact in your life journey.
- *Mentoring*—making an emotional, spiritual, and physical deposit of seeds into someone's life to impact their *season* in life.
- *Mentoring*—pouring your love for God into another. They will begin to see His mission for their lives and, hopefully, will become obedient to His missions call.

raised by an extended family. This makes mentoring by Christian women an urgent and increasingly important ministry.

Life would never again be the same in Nazareth . . . especially for young Mary, the mother of Jesus. Surely, she hung on the words of the angel, Gabriel: "The Lord is with you. Do not be afraid, Mary, for you have found favor with God."

Can you imagine how, as she headed for the hill country with haste to visit Elizabeth, she repeated, "Do not be afraid, Mary. Do not be afraid, Mary." Ken Medema, the singer/songwriter, portrays so vividly what she must have been thinking in her young mind: "So many things are happening to me that I don't understand. . . . Plans that I'd made are like bird's nests, blowing in the wind and rain. . . . So I'll go tell Elizabeth. She'll understand. . . . She'll hold my hand. She'll understand."

*It's a woman thing!* I have come to know Carleen Ozley through letters and materials. She responded to my recent questionnaire about mentoring. I've taken five of her thoughts and interspersed them with my thoughts about Mary and Elizabeth. Carleen calls it spiritual mentoring rather than spiritual mothering because many women who had less-than-good mother role models might be turned away from the very thing they want and need. Carleen ministers to women through a local church in Birmingham, Alabama, and in a written interview shared these thoughts:

*1. As women, we are created with a unique nurturing need. God is the source and sustainer and focus of all relationships. As women, we have been given the capacity for nurturing for the purpose of glorifying God.*

Mary was certainly in need of that kind of nurturing. She must have hoped that Elizabeth would understand what was happening to her and would give her guidance and wisdom.

*2. Women today live in a transient and mobile society—our economic situation keeps us on the move and we go wherever the job is.*

Certainly, this points to the need for mentoring, perhaps even more today. As we are constantly on the move, the church, and in particular women, need to reach out quickly and take the risk of starting a relationship with a new neighbor . . . new office worker . . . new patient in the doctor's office . . . or new church member. They might not be there very long.

Mary and Joseph experienced moving about during Jesus' early life. I imagine the *she'll understand* part of Mary and Elizabeth's mentoring relationship kept them in touch with each other, drawing strength from each other in day-to-day living. After all, they both pondered deep things in their hearts about God's work in the lives of their sons.

Seasons of life may be experienced in weeks or years. Don't let self-imposed time restraints keep you from beginning a mentoring friendship! My dearest friendship is with Jo Vaughn. We have been sharing life for more than 33 years—and we're not through yet! On the other hand, I was blessed for 18 months by the life of a godly retired woman in the winter of her life, whose voice, demeanor, and physical presence reflected the Spirit of Christ. We served on a committee together. Aubrey Edward Johns brought spring into the autumn of my life. I flowered during that time, inspired by her walk with God. She was always showing me His fragrance in her life. I was inspired to be more gentle and quiet because of viewing her garden life of gentleness and calmness. Let's give ourselves permission to form short-term mentoring relationships.

*3. Women need women to communicate in the language of the heart and feelings. We are all talkers and have a need to send our thoughts and feelings to a receiver of like mind.*

Mary and Elizabeth shared the language of the heart. But they went further—they shared the language and feeling of God's heart! Spiritual depth is the foundation for Christian mentoring!

Mary's first thoughts were, *How can this be?* She had heard the stories from childhood about the coming Messiah, and what mother had not longed for her daughter to be chosen to bear God's Son! Susan Hunt's book, *Spiritual Mothering*, gives us insight:

> Suddenly, without warning, Mary was hurled from the quiet life of small town obscurity to a succession of emotional highs and lows. Consider the staggering extremes:
> - astonishment at seeing an angel.
> - exhilaration upon hearing that she had been chosen to carry the Son of God in her womb.
> - anxiety about how her fiancé would accept such news.
> - confusion concerning the legitimate question of how such a physical impossibility could take place since she was a virgin.
> - fear of the possible consequences of rejection and shame.[1]

The angel answered her thoughts, and in Luke 1:28, 35 (NIV), brought her these words: "Greetings, you who are highly favored! The Lord is with you. . . . The Holy Spirit will come upon you, and the power of the Most High will overshadow you."

The Greek word *favor* means grace. Mary's humble faith led to her acceptance of God's grace to her, enabling her childlike response . . . "be it done to me according to your word" (Luke 1:38 NASB). Note that Mary first trusted God in the situation; then turned to Elizabeth. It was her faith that gave her a strong purpose at such a young age. We are asked for that kind of faith and purpose, and we have the same grace available in our lives as we mentor with a passion to bring glory to God.

We do not know the relationship that Mary and Elizabeth had prior to the announcement of the angel. We can wonder if they confided about Mary's upcoming marriage. Had they talked about having children? If so, how many? Had they talked about the work of their husbands and their places in the community? There must have been a close relationship between them because the Scripture says Mary left *with haste* for Elizabeth's home.

A dear friend? Yes! A relative may be a close friend. How rich for both! Probably neither one dreamed all that God was about to do in and through their lives. What affirmation Mary received when she announced her condition to Elizabeth! She heard no condemnation and no hard questions—just pure faith in God's plan. The baby in Elizabeth's womb jumped for joy at Mary's announcement. Now their friendship was bound together in God's almighty plan. What a great season God was bringing into their lives. Though different ages, they were connected because of God's agenda. After the initial excitement of the news and the time of worship as Mary sang praise to God, they must have sat down together.

- As they held each other, did they laugh and weep together? Of course, they did! *It's a woman thing!*
- Did they make eternal promises to each other about the long journey ahead? Surely they did—that's what sisters do.
- Did they promise to stick together when no one else understood or accepted God's plan? Yes, because they shared the language of the heart—as only women can share with each other.

*4. Acceptance and encouragement are needed by women and are best given by women.*

*5. The most appealing and satisfying aspect of a mentoring relationship is that it is not program-based, list-dictated, but lived out in the context of the RELATIONSHIP of our daily lives.*

Carleen is now mentoring a young woman who has been a friend of mine for several years. She said to me: "Since you know Alisha, it will come as no surprise for me to tell you that our relationship is my delight! I am blessed to walk with her, pray for her, and watch as God is making Himself known in her and through her." In mentoring, we may find ourselves sharing seasons with other mentors and mentees.

These points serve to underscore the importance of women mentoring women. Mentoring, an active and powerful form of discipleship, has been neglected among sisters in Christ for too long.

## Young Women in Search of a Mentor
Determine your needs in this season of your life.

- Do you need a listener . . . a coach . . . or an encourager?
- Do you want to sharpen your leadership skills or your parenting skills?
- Do you have goals and aspirations?
- Who among your friends can help you reach your goals and aspirations?
- Whom do you respect and admire in leadership? a relative? a neighbor? a Bible teacher in the city? a retired schoolteacher? a grandmother?

Ask yourself these two questions:

1. Of these people, with whom would I like to spend time?

Once you have decided with whom you would like to spend time, pick up the phone and call that person to see if a mentoring relationship is possible. Write a note to the prospective mentor stating your goals, and ask to be considered as a mentee. Ask if you could have 30 minutes on the phone every other week, or get together for coffee once a month, or whatever arrangement might be viable and suitable for both parties.

If that person does not have the time or if you sense a lack of interest, ask if they know of someone who might be willing to help you.

2. What community programs are offered?

Check your community news to see what classes or seminars are offered in your area. This is a great way to learn a skill and at the same time, find a person with similar interests—and perhaps, a mentor. Mentors can be found inside and outside the church community!

## Older Women in Search of a Mentee

Determine your needs in this season of your life.
- Do you need a listener . . . or a friend?
- Do you want to learn new skills?
- Do you have a desire to come alongside and help someone?
- Do you or your friends know a young single mother who needs a grandmother?
- Whom do you respect and admire in leadership? Is it a young or middle-aged relative? a neighbor who needs encouragement? a Bible teacher in the city for whom you could pray? a

woman who needs to attend a program at the community college for whom you could provide child care? a retired schoolteacher who is looking for a travel companion for a short trip?

Ask yourself these two questions:

1. Of these people, with whom would I like to spend time?
   Once you have decided with whom you would like to spend time, pick up the phone and call that person. Ask if you can help or be of assistance. Write a note to the prospective mentee, offering to be a phone friend every other week.

2. What community programs are offered?
   What a great way to learn a skill and find a person of like interest—and, perhaps, a mentee. Remember: mentees can be found outside the church community!

## It's a Heavenly Plan

I was 16 years old, attending a church camp in Mount Baker, Washington, when I first met Margaret Sisemore. She was instructing adults how to teach the Bible. I found myself sitting in her classes every day that week because she was so different from any Christian I had ever met before. I now know it was the fragrance of Christ that permeated her life and drew me into her life garden.

What a difference she has made in my life! I followed her everywhere during that week of camp, wanting to be near her and to hear everything she said. When the week was over, she took me aside and her words to me changed my life: "Esther, God has something for you to do. It is something no one else can do. Don't forget that!"

Then, she prayed with me. Her words rang in my heart throughout the next year! At a youth rally the following spring, I obediently submitted my life to God for special ministry. In the truest sense, Margaret has been my mentor throughout my life. Through these years, it has been a long-distance relationship by phone calls, encouraging notes, and personal visits. Margaret, and her late husband, John, did not have children. She claimed me and my husband, Bob, as her special kids.

In most recent years as I have traveled across the United States teaching and speaking, she would send clippings from the papers that crossed her desk and include an encouraging note. I remember the first time she heard me speak. I was more than nervous; but she sat out there beaming with parental pride, smiling, encouraging me with her face.

I later asked if she was nervous when she first began speaking. She assured me that she had been very nervous; but she pretended she wasn't nervous at all until she got over it! We laughed together, knowing the real truth. When I first began speaking, my father mentored me with these words, "If you're not a little bit scared every time you get up to speak, you're not trusting Him completely."

Margaret Sisemore saw in me what I could not see in myself, and her vision was so clear. She dreamed a dream with me until I could begin to see what she could see—and what God would see in the garden of my life. God desires for you, dear reader, to consider joining His plan for women in the task of the mentoring.

## Selecting a Mentee

1. Begin with prayer. Ask God to show you who needs to be mentored by you.
2. Be intentional about selecting a mentee and mentoring her. Think through the possibilities of what you might accomplish together before you approach her.
3. Don't allow age to limit your selection.
4. Women have so much to offer as mentors! You can do it!

# II

## *What Grows Here?*

Once you have decided where you want to plant your garden, stop and take a look at what is already growing there. You don't want to dig up and discard everything already growing. If there are plants there that please you, you may want to work them into your complete plan. Other plants may be less desirable: those that spread quickly, choking out other plants; poisonous plants; those that just don't fit the broader scheme.

### How Do I Approach This Potential Mentee?

Carefully and prayerfully! You have prayed about whom God would have you select. Now ask God to guide you as you approach her.

If you are not already acquainted, establish casual contact with this person. Invite her—and her family, if she has one—to dinner one weekend. If she doesn't work outside the home, invite her to have coffee or tea with you after everyone else leaves in the morning. Find other ways to interact with her.

When God leads you to the person you should mentor, call her on Monday morning, after the little ones are settled or after she gets to work, and inquire about how you can pray for her during the week. Call her back a week later and ask her, "What has God done?" You will be teaching her of God's power, your concern, and the fragrance of Christ as you invest in her life. You will be teaching her to join you in prayer for her family and friends and to live in the expectancy of what God will do. What a fragrance to God this will be! What a fragrance of encouragement this will be to her. Begin with prayer!

### Informal or Formal Mentoring

At some point, you'll need to decide if you want to be involved in an informal or a formal mentoring relationship. In an informal mentoring relationship, you develop a friendship rather than a formal learning environment. The only difference between a mentoring friendship and any other friendship is your own intentionality. You work at a mentoring friendship to help another woman develop mentally, spiritually, and physically. You should have a plan on paper—some written record of the things you see in your mentee's life and the ways in which you are encouraging her to develop. However, this record is not something that you would show your mentee; it is a guide to keep you intentional about mentoring. Along the way you'll find you've made a good friend, but that can't be your sole purpose.

A formal mentoring relationship involves much more structure. In an informal mentoring relationship, you have a plan that you probably will not show to your mentee. In a formal mentoring relationship, you and the mentee will draw up and occasionally evaluate a plan together. You will still develop a special friendship and do lots of fun things together, but both you and your mentee take an active interest in developing a plan that will help your mentee grow.

Informal mentoring relationships can become formal mentoring relationships, but that is something you'll have to play by ear. Your mentee may request a formal mentoring relationship. It will be an indication of growth and maturity on her part, showing that she has developed a sense of direction and purpose and that she feels you can help her achieve her goals. Or, you may want to approach your mentee. If you begin to sense that formal mentoring relationship would be beneficial to your mentee, prayerfully approach her about it. Be prepared to accept her answer, whatever it may be, without allowing a negative response to affect your current relationship.

## The First Meeting

Whether your mentoring relationship is formal or informal, your first meeting should be a very positive and affirming meeting. Meet over coffee or lunch. Be honest and tell her that you have noticed her. Describe what it was that first made you notice her. Tell her that you have seen great ability and even greater potential in her. Don't flatter her; just be open and honest about what you have seen in her.

If this is to be an informal mentoring relationship, this will be the first of many times you will get together in an informal and friendly setting. You'll talk about life, goals, problems, and other things. You'll pray together, study the Bible together, laugh together, and cry together.

If you are planning a formal mentoring relationship, after you have prayed about her, for her, and with her on several occasions, set up a time to talk to your mentee about mentoring. Tell her that you have seen something special in her, and that you feel led to discuss it with her. Ask if she would be willing to meet with you. Describe your desire to be involved in mentoring. Tell her you would enjoy helping her develop, if she is interested. If she is interested, set up another time to meet and discuss a mentoring plan.

From this point on, little distinction will be made between formal and informal mentoring. You should note, however, that there are two fundamental differences between the formal and the informal mentoring relationship: time and planning.

In the informal relationship, progress may take more time. You can't sit down in a meeting and say, "OK. Today let's outline your goals and define the habits that keep you from achieving them." You'll have to be more subtle in drawing out the information you need to form a plan. Over lunch one day, you may talk about your goals in life and then ask her about hers. The next time you meet you may be able to find out what kinds of things she is doing that take her closer to her goal. Several lunch dates later, you may be able to find out what hinders her progress toward her goals. But this, and any other information you need, will have to be discovered through casual conversation.

You may eventually develop the type of relationship with your mentee in which you can ask your mentee to outline her goals and other things; but once you begin to gather information in this way, you begin a gradual transition into a formal process. The blending of the two styles of mentoring can be good. The style you use will vary from situation to situation.

The other difference is in how you plan. In an informal situation, you'll have to wait until you're alone to make notes from your meeting. The plans you develop won't be formally shared with your mentee.

In spite of these differences, both formal and informal mentoring follow a similar process.

## What Already Grows in Your Mentor's Life

Once you have established a mentor-mentee relationship, the two of you should stop and take a long look at her life. Some of what you see in her life needs to stay and be nourished and encouraged to grow. Other things that you see may not belong in her life.

What do you see growing in your mentee's life? What does she see growing in her life? Are there things in her life that should not be there? What are they? Together, make a list of those things. The list will serve as a guide when you and your mentee begin to plan.

Now, together decide what grows in your mentee's life that is good. Are there characteristics, desires, habits, and other things that should be nourished and encouraged to grow? What are these things? Make a list.

Also ask yourself, *What do I see in her life that she cannot see now?* What she does not see may hinder her more than anything else in her life. If your mentee has unconscious characteristics or habits that are hindering her progress in life, your ability to see and point these problem areas out may be difficult for her to accept. Your ability to approach her thoughtfully and prayerfully is of prime importance.

Your mentee may be hindered even more by the good characteristics or traits that she does not see in her life. As human beings and especially as women, we are hard on ourselves. It is usually very easy to see what is wrong with us and incredibly difficult to spot what is good in us. As a mentor, you have the responsibility for spotting what is good in your mentee and drawing it out of her. Help her to reach the potential that she is not even aware is hers. Think back to the person in your life who saw in you what you did not see in yourself. This person helped water and nourish your life, encouraged the seeds of your gifts and uniqueness, and helped you to blossom into the person you have now become.

Cindy Walker Gaskins became a part of our family as she baby-sat and encouraged our children during my last few years as the campus minister at Samford University in Birmingham, Alabama. I could see incredible leadership skills in this young woman—such a reliance on God in her daily walk and such joy in life. As she joined the campus ministry leadership team, active in many areas, I shared my dream for her to become the campus ministry president before she graduated. In her senior year, Cindy was elected as the campus ministry president at Samford University.

I still remember her surprise when I asked her to consider

praying about putting her name on the ballot. After all, she was *a woman*. My response was, "Why not? You are the most qualified."

In the spring of that year, I moved to Atlanta to begin a new job. No one was better prepared to finish out the year than Cindy. Her four years of serving on the team stretched her gifts and gave her confidence as a leader. Cindy might never have realized her full potential without a little encouragement. The same can be said of almost everyone. We all need a little encouragement. We all need to have someone point out the good in us and help us reach for the dreams we have never dared to dream.

What grows already in your mentee's life?

## The Initial Approach

1. Observe your mentee carefully. What is already growing in her life, both good and bad?
2. Now ask yourself, *What can I see in her that she cannot see?*
3. Pray. Ask God to guide you as you approach her about a mentee/mentor relationship.
4. Decide whether an informal or formal mentoring relationship would be best.
5. Establish casual contact first, if you are not already acquainted. Invite her to coffee or lunch occasionally.
6. Ask what she wants you to pray about. Call her the following week to find out what God has done.
7. After much prayer, set up a time to talk to her about mentoring, if your relationship is to be a formal one.

# III

## *Plotting the Possibilities*

"Many gardeners have a tendency at this point to look for spots for their favorite flowers, rather than looking for flowers that fit the site. . . . While you're planning your garden, keep your mind open to the possibilities."[1]

Ask God to help you envision a mentoring garden. James 1:5 (NIV) instructs us, "If any of you lacks wisdom, he should ask God, who gives generously to all without finding fault, and it will be given to him."

Wisdom is the process of discernment in which choices are weighed. For a Christian woman, these choices are always made in keeping with God's desires. We can ask God for wisdom and, according to His promise, He will give it.

After buying every garden magazine I could find and dreaming about the kind of garden I would have, I put together bits and pieces from different garden settings and listed the flowers and bushes I desired to plant. As I planned my garden, I consulted a landscape expert for advice. I showed him several of the designs I had found.

A lot of dreaming and planning went into my garden long before I began to prepare the garden bed. Mentoring is much like gardening. It takes time, patience, and expert advice. In mentoring, you'll dream, plan, and work hard, but don't neglect to consult the Master Gardener each step of the way. Bathe all you do in prayer and seek wisdom from God.

### First Steps in Planning

One of the first steps in plotting a garden is to take everything into account that will affect your garden. How much sunlight does the area receive? What is the lay of the land—hilly, rocky, flat, wet? What are the obstacles in the area—any trees, buildings, fences, pathways?

Discuss the following with your mentee:

- How much *Sonlight* does your life's garden receive?
- How does your life currently lay? What direction are you currently heading? Are you heading that way as part of a plan? Or are you just growing wild, allowing whichever plant is strongest to take over your life?
- What are the obstacles in your life? If you are not getting enough exposure to the Son of God, what obstacles can be removed so that your garden receives more Sonlight? What are the obstacles that hinder the growth of desirable plants in your life's garden? Can they be removed, or do we have to work around them?

If your mentee is not a Christian, you will need to be sensitive about which spiritual questions to leave out for now. Spiritual questions may be better discussed in prayer between you and God for the time being.

The question of purpose must also be decided:

- What do I desire in and from this investment?
- What do I wish to accomplish through this mentoring relationship?
- What do you expect from me?

Begin by setting the boundaries of the mentor/mentee relationship. Both of you should state clearly what you expect from the relationship. State your expectations and give your mentee a chance to state her expectations. In this way, boundaries will be set and you will both feel more comfortable with the process.

Here are some questions you might discuss with your mentee:

- What are our goals?
- What attitudes can be taught and learned?
- What characteristics do you have upon which we can build?
- What do I see in you that you may not see?
- What are my spiritual gifts?
- What are your spiritual gifts? (Ask this if she is a Christian; if not move to the next set of questions.)

These questions will bring definition to your mentoring relationship. However, in this shared journey, each of you will need to keep redefining your expectations as you continue to grow and work through life experiences together.

In 1 Thessalonians 2:8*a* (NIV), we read: "We loved you so much that we were delighted to share with you not only the gospel of God but our lives as well." You will be sharing both the light of Christ as well as your life in this mentoring relationship.

Through discussion with your mentee, find out what her goals and dreams are. Where does she see herself a few years from now? What will she be doing? Dream the dream with her and help her walk through the following questions:

- If I could change anything in my life, what would it be?
- If I can't change it, how can I work around it or turn it to my advantage?
- If I can change it, how will I go about it?

## What Should Be Planted?

It is so much fun to look at all the possibilities! You'll look through lots of seed catalogs and gardening magazines. You'll *ooh!* and *aah!* over certain plants. You'll dog-ear the corners of the pages showing your favorites, or you'll cut and paste your favorites together, as I did! What fun planning can be!

Dream about the possibilities. Take a look at your mentee's life, and ask the following questions:

- What seeds should I plant in this person? A love of Sonlight? A passion for spreading seeds—missions? An ability to nurture others—mothering skills? What about prayer and how to pray more effectively?
- What kinds of plants will give her life's garden the look that the Master Gardener desires?

As you study the Bible and pray together, you will be able to determine the answers to these questions. And, as you and your mentee dream about other possibilities for her life, together you'll discover many other seeds that need to be planted.

What character traits or habits need to be planted? What about seeds of balance, trust, caring, courage, listening,and guidance?

Does your mentee have career or educational goals? What are they? Help her to dream about the possibilities and, together, search for the seeds that will help her achieve her goals. Both of you should read articles about the career she has chosen. Look through college catalogs together. Dream together and help her to reach beyond what she currently believes is possible.

Is she a wife or a mother who has goals for changing or improving the way her household is run? Or is she retired and searching for new ways to make life meaningful? Look at all the possibilities. Help her to find books that suggest new possibilities.

*The Secret Garden* is a wonderful story of grace. As the story unfolds, the garden is found, life is rediscovered, and in the process, every person at Misselthwaite Manor is changed in some way. They blossom, share gifts, and together, make a garden bouquet with the fragrance of friendship and community. In the story, Mary and Colin slowly become friends. She reads to him, enlarging his world and awakening his desire to read good books and to experience life. In the process of the friendship, she can't help sharing her love for gardening, animals, nature, and things. One day, Colin responds to Mary's joy in life with these haunting words: "I wish I were friends with things."

I have always been friends with *things*. Miniature dollhouses, flower gardens, and needlework are part of my family heritage and treasure. I enjoy things, especially books that talk. You might ask, *What do you mean, Esther? Books that talk?* Well, while reading have you ever said aloud, *Yes! That's right.* Then you underline and make notes in the margin, noting the truth you have read and embraced from your own experience. I call that listening and talking back to a book. Haven't you ever left tearstains as well as the echo of your laughter in a book because the written word so deeply touched your heart? I have.

Gardens touch our lives. So do people. People talk. Gardens listen. Books do both. Books are friends in my life, and have been enormous mentors in my spiritual formation and lifestyle.

Not long ago, I was privileged to be part of a women's conference in Ohio. One of the keynote speakers was Jill Briscoe. Cindy Landry, the chairperson for the meeting, invited Jill and me to lunch upon our arrival. I was delighted. I knew about Jill through her teaching and books and very much admired her ministry with women, but had never met her. As soon as we were seated and the introductions made, Cindy turned to Jill and said these words:

"I want to thank you for being a mentor in my life, even though I have not met you until today. As a young minister's wife, I was really struggling with time priorities, parenting, and wanting my husband to be home more and do things with me. In that struggle, I found your book, *There's a Snake in My Garden*, and it changed my life. I am so glad to get the opportunity to thank you in person."

What a treasure for Cindy to meet the author who mentored her with the written word.

To hide away with a book is as vital to a soul as water is to a plant, . . . as music is to a heart, . . . as a friend is to a life. Books have the ability to change lives or *to turn things around.* Some books weed and prune, while others encourage and affirm. I have a shelf in my office that contains my favorite life-altering books. These books are friends that I value and keep in close reach. I reread them often. I could not list all of them, but let me share one that is next to my Bible and has been life-altering for me.

I am the most spiritually challenged by Oswald Chambers's classic devotional guide, *My Utmost for His Highest.* I have worn out more than one copy. I have thrown it down many times, declaring, "This is too hard!" Henry Blackaby once told me, "When you read a book, you know about the author. When you read Oswald Chambers, you know about God." Year after year, Chambers's daily writings have carried me in my quest to know God better. He never allows self-indulgence, but rather, through the Scripture, he points toward giving your utmost for God's highest purpose. This book is part of my daily journal and the margins are full of notes—reminders of dates and situations in which I've come before God with my heart crushed in conviction or celebratory in adoration. Oswald Chambers, from another generation, has been a mentor in my life.

All that to say, books can open up a world of possibilities for your mentee. Introduce her to books that will expand her view of the possibilities for her life's garden. Introduce new dreams to her life. Introduce new ways to solve old problems.

Through conversation, through books and magazines, through Bible study and prayer—in these and other ways, you'll begin to see a garden plan unfold. The Master Gardener will help you select those seeds that are most suited for the life garden of your mentee.

# IV
## *It's a Plan!*

You've picked the perfect garden site, decided which plants stay and which ones go, and looked at all the possibilities. Now it's time to draw up your plan. Put it down on paper. What seeds will you plant? When? Where?

## Choosing the Seeds

Look back through your catalogs at those dog-eared pages. What were your favorite plants? If you are like me, you'll have to make some tough decisions. Nevertheless, if you'll narrow your focus and pick only the best seeds, your garden will be even more beautiful than if you had planted everything that you found appealing.

"They left everything and followed Him" (Luke 5:11*b* NASB).

Jesus chose to plant His life in the lives of the Twelve Disciples. When you think about it that was quite an undertaking. Into the soil of the lives of these 12 men, Jesus chose to plant the seeds of faith through:

- example;
- teaching;
- correction;
- serving;
- loving;

. . . to lead His mission. He chose unique and individualistic seeds for His harvest field. Under His tutelage, their strengths and weaknesses blended and flowered in community. It seems the Master Teacher had a way of working the soil of their hearts to show them Kingdom authority and to produce Kingdom fruit.

The Ultimate Mentor is Jesus, divinely focused on God's purpose for His life. He came to plant the love of God through redemption. On His way to the cross, Jesus took the Twelve He chose to mentor, while adding many others to His ministry team, and trusted them with the work of His Kingdom.

Imagine a CEO today, in search of some new employees, walking by the lake near the business. She hires a couple of fishermen with no résumés or recommendations—on the spot—to lead in the business! You're right—it wouldn't happen!

Under the mentoring of Christ, this motley crew and the host of other disciples became the movers and shakers of their time—with continued impact on our time—through the power of the Holy Spirit.

- Peter . . . *the rock*
- Barnabas . . . *the encourager*
- Mary and Martha . . . *compassionate friends*
- Mark . . . *the encourager of suffering Christians*
- Luke . . . *the defender of women and children*
- Andrew . . . *the evangelist*

A host of others were changed by Jesus' mentoring leadership, and they became change agents in their culture. Jesus taught them everything His Father had taught Him. He then modeled Kingdom living. In John 14:12 (NASB), He promised: "Truly, truly, I say to you, he who believes in Me, the works that I do shall he do also; and greater works than these shall he do; because I go to the Father."

Your first reaction is perhaps like mine: *How could I ever do anything greater than Jesus?* I've never brought anyone from death back to life. I've never given someone their sight—unless of course, I share the gospel with someone who has been blinded by sin and introduce them to new life in Christ. Jesus completed His work on the cross. God, the Father, now accomplishes His work through the power of the Holy Spirit in and through obedient Christians, just as He did at Pentecost. The Ultimate Mentor drew up alongside His disciples, pouring Himself into their lives, showing them how to teach, to heal, to bless, to forgive, and to pour themselves into the lives of others.

In the summer of 1995, I had the privilege of taking part in the Pastor's School at Beeson Divinity School, Samford University. The Bible teacher for the week was Warren W. Wiersbe. It is from his teaching that week that I present some thoughts for

your consideration. Wiersbe taught from the parables in
Matthew. In describing parables as pictures, he said this: "The
longer you look at the parable picture in Scripture, it starts to
turn into a mirror and you begin to see yourself. Look again
and the mirror becomes a window and you see God."

*Wow!* I'm in the picture! And then it dawns on me—God is in
the picture with me! Matthew 13:18–23 is a story about the
sower, the soil, and the harvest. In *The Message,* the harvest
story reads like this:

> Study this story of the farmer planting seed. When any-
> one hears news of the kingdom and doesn't take it in,
> it just remains on the surface, and so the Evil One
> comes along and plucks it right out of that person's
> heart. This is the seed the farmer scatters on the road.
>
> The seed cast in the gravel—this is the person who
> hears and instantly responds with enthusiasm. But
> there is no soil of character, and so when the emotions
> wear off and some difficulty arrives, there is nothing to
> show for it.
>
> The seed cast in the weeds is the person who hears
> the kingdom news, but weeds of worry and illusions
> about getting more and wanting everything under the
> sun strangle what was heard, and nothing comes of it.
>
> The seed cast on good earth is the person who
> hears and takes in the News, and then produces a
> harvest beyond his wildest dreams.

The picture shows us that the seed is the Word of God, and
we must trust the Word. Why do you think that the Word of
God would be compared to seed? Seeds have life in them, and
so does the Word of God.

Matthew 13:23 (NASB) says, "And the one on whom seed
was sown on the good soil, this is the man who hears the word
and understands it; who indeed bears fruit, and brings forth,
some a hundredfold, some sixty, and some thirty."

Most seeds are small and may look insignificant—that is, until
the seed is placed in the ground, dies, and then comes to life in
the nutrient rich soil. The Word of God planted in a woman's
life is the source of power for life. It is trusting in the God-
breathed Word that we experience the Spirit's power.

When Jesus plants the Word, it has the power to change from the inside out. Just to carry the Word or to have it on a coffee table will not change us. But planted in our hearts, we embrace it and live in its power.

One must plant seeds that develop into characteristics of spiritual leadership. One must teach the mentee about unconditional love, grace, and discipline.

## Seeds Families Should Plant

Colossians 2:6–7 (NASB) says, "As you therefore have received Christ Jesus the Lord, so walk in Him, having been firmly rooted and now being built up in Him and established in your faith, just as you were instructed, and overflowing with gratitude."

With families who are walking in and deeply rooted in Christ, mentoring is natural and comes from the overflowing gratitude. Families can easily plant the following seeds:

- work
- patience
- hope
- joy
- success
- beauty
- positive response to failure

As I planted my garden, I wanted beauty—a balance of annuals and perennials, as well as ground cover, beautiful plants, and color in different seasons. Remember: as you pick your seeds and plan your garden, you want to develop balance, color, and beauty in the mentee's life, and that takes careful and disciplined planning.

Some plants have spectacular flowers, but the length of time they flower is very short. They look beautiful but only for a brief time. I personally would rather invest in plants that flower all summer, such as daisies and moss rose.

I think the same is true for the gardening life of the mentor and mentee. Go for depth and beauty, planting the roots in deep, rather than surface beauty that looks spectacular but may not be long lasting. We want the seeds to reproduce a hundred-fold, so make good investments in your seed.

Besides the Word of God, spiritual depth, and a beautiful character, you will plant ideas and vision. You will seek to inspire your mentee, to help her reach for the good things which may seem beyond her grasp. You will plant seeds that help her grow as a leader, a mother, a daughter, a sister, a friend, a wife, a student—seeds that will help her reach her potential as a Christian woman. However, unless you have planted the Word of God in her along with spiritual depth and a beautiful character, the other plants that grow in her life will have no visual anchor, no background against which to blossom and grow. They will appear lost. Anchor any other seeds you plant in the Word of God, in spiritual depth, and in beauty of character.

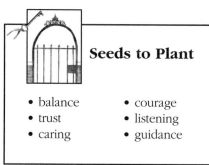

**Seeds to Plant**

- balance
- trust
- caring
- courage
- listening
- guidance

## Long-Range and Short-Range Planning

When designing a garden, you don't need to do everything the first year if you have a long-range plan.

For the most part, the disciples got it! Jesus really meant *follow me.* Jesus chose people He felt could replace Him. If you choose to become a mentor, your assignment is to work yourself out of a job! Even more correct might be to work someone else into a job or a call. That's your long-range plan—to serve your mentee so well that they in turn learn what it means to serve and begin serving others. You want to turn things around in your mentee's life. But more than that, you want her to produce seeds that will be planted in other gardens.

Laurie Beth Jones, author of *Jesus CEO,* says this:

> In almost every situation in which Jesus found Himself, His job was to turn things around. In fact, that was His specialty.

- The people here have forgotten Who I am! Turn this around!
- There is a little girl dying here! Turn this around!
- People are dishonoring the temple! Turn this around!

Jones also says that Jesus didn't come to give us a new formula. He came to give us a new mind-set—one that has a turnaround mentality. Turnaround specialists are really turnaround artists. Don't mark yourself off the list because of the word *specialist*. Many of you certainly are specialists and don't even know it! *Webster's* defines the word *artist* like this: "one who is skilled in any of the fine arts." An artisan is a skilled craftsperson.

Mentors are skilled in helping a mentee turn things around in their own lives first, and then, in the lives of others. Gardeners are also skilled at turning things around.

I'm proud to announce that my small English garden is finally complete! What joy has been mine to plant the seeds that define its beauty—well, at least, to watch Bob plant those seeds! I was the garden director, you understand! Looking at the garden three months later, I am amazed everyday at the changing beauty.

- The moss rose creeps over the rocks—with no regard for any other plant in its way. I'll change that around next season!
- The purple salvia began with three small plants and has now tripled in size. I won't turn that around! I like their place in my garden.
- The yellow lantana will have to be turned around next spring, moving from the front to the back of the garden. It will look better there, near the rock wall, as if to frame the weeping willow.

Short-range goals are just as important as long-range goals. Your short-range goals may change as the seeds planted in your mentee begin to blossom. Just as I can see changes that need to be made in my garden plan, you will see changes that need to be made in your mentoring garden plan. Adjust. Set new short-range goals and allow the warmth of the Son to bring out the best in your mentee's life garden.

Your long-range goals won't change, but what you plan in the short term will have to change to enable you and your mentee to meet those goals.

## Putting Pen to Paper

Some years ago, Bob and I wrote a song whose lyrics continue
to haunt me. It is titled, "We Can Change Things Around."

Lord, what if I became a servant?
By forgiving and not grudging
By accepting, not rejecting
And by healing and not hurting
I can change things around.

Lord, what if I became a servant?
By bending and not bowing
By giving and not taking
And by list'ning and not talking
I can change things around.

Lord, what if I became a servant?
By sharing, not indulging
By selecting, not collecting
And by serving, not demanding
I can change things around.

We can change things around . . .
with a serving heart.
We can change things around . . .
we'll do our part . . .
We can change things around.
© 1990 B&E Productions

Mentoring is helping set directions which *can change things
around*. To choose to mentor will change some things because
mentoring takes time and effort by both parties. Some mentoring
will be affirming the place in which the mentee finds herself in
this season of life.

Recently, Bob and I decided it was time to get new eyeglasses
and at our age, that meant a full examination and lens changes. I
moved to bifocals and he moved to trifocals. I admit, sometimes
I will wear half glasses just to help the contacts a bit.

One morning, Bob came into the kitchen pointing to his eyes,
and asked me, "What's this?"

"Bags," I responded.

"Well, how long have they been there?" he asked in surprise. "And how did they get there?"

I know I should not have laughed. But when you don't wear your glasses on a regular basis, you can't see the bags. What a great way to live! But it also means that most of the time, I have to help him by reading the phone book, menus, and anything that is in small print. I've placed six pairs of drugstore half glasses around our house and none are *ever* in the right room at the right time. *It's a man thing!* We laugh about this.

When drawing up a mentoring plan, we must have a clear and eternal focus—even more clear than when using trifocals!

Many gardening books tell gardeners to keep a monthly journal in order to keep on track with the constant needs of a garden. A March list might look like this:

- sow seeds in pots and flats
- complete garden pruning
- repair garden wall
- fertilize trees and shrubs
- remove mulch
- aerate lawn and reseed where necessary

Your May journal entries might read:

- transplanted annuals
- fed roses
- weeding continued as necessary
- fertilized new seedlings lightly
- picked bouquets for guests

The list tells me that this gardener knows what she is doing and what she has to accomplish to fully enjoy the fruit of her labors. Gardeners must know when to fertilize, water, and care for each plant and vegetable in order to enhance its growth.

Mentors learn what it takes to enhance the growth of the mentee in each individual situation. As the mentor works on this relationship, *nurturing* is a good word to keep in mind. Just as the soil needs nutrients to enhance growth in plants and to produce fruit, mentees need nurturing and enhancing.

Starting with a mentoring plan and keeping continuous records will enable you to stay focused and clear. You will have a record of the gardening tricks that worked and those that did not. You'll have a record of what has been done, and following your plan, you'll know what comes next. Write out your plan, keep good records, and stay clearly focused.

The mentoring relationship is going to take strong commitment and steady work. Mentors and mentees can enjoy watching their seeds come to life, grow strong, and finally, produce good fruit. Bobb Biehl, in his book *Mentoring*, says this: "Mentoring should be seen as a partnership between two persons for the purpose of mutual growth."

## It's a Plan!

1. Choose carefully what you will plant.
2. Be sure to include the seeds of the Word of God, spiritual depth, and beauty of character.
3. Have a long-range plan—to create a garden in your mentee's life that will grow, blossom, and produce new seeds to plant in the life of another.
4. Have short-range plans which are flexible and change as necessary to enhance growth toward the long-range goal.
5. Write your plan down and keep records. This will enable you to stay focused on the long-range goal.
6. Set a time to terminate or reevaluate the mentoring relationship. This will enable either one of you to gracefully back out of the relationship if it is bad—or to refocus as growth takes place.

# Part Two
# Cultivating and Sowing

# V

## *Working the Soil*

"You didn't choose me, remember; I chose you, and put you in the world to bear fruit, fruit that won't spoil. As fruit bearers, whatever you ask the Father in relation to me, he gives you" (John 15:16 *The Message*).

"Is there anything you want?"

"Might I," quavered Mary, "might I have a bit of earth?"

Mr. Craven says, "You can have as much earth as you want. When you see a bit of earth you want, take it, child, and make it come alive."[1]

In the book, *The Secret Garden*, the main character, Mary Lennox, finally meets the master of the house, who is her uncle, Mr. Craven. He had no idea what a spectacular garden would come forth in Mary's life. The impact would be so positive, it would change everyone in the household. Working in garden soil and planting roots deep give stability and strength to the plant. In some ways, this is similar to the choosing of a mentoring relationship—it takes work and risk to make the relationship come alive and, perhaps, change the whole world.

### Make the Garden Bed

I have a friend who planted some seeds in a pot. The plant sprouted and quickly wilted! Her gardener friend, observing that pitiful little plant, asked what kind of soil she used. My friend responded, "Soil from the backyard. Isn't that OK?"

It wasn't. Most garden beds need to be prepared before they can receive seeds and nurture them. Working the soil is a vital part of the gardening process.

Without bed preparation, little fruit will result. My father, a master gardener and still gardening at age 90, told me this about working the soil:

- Remove the stones or other obstacles.
- Prepare the soil for those seeds you have decided to plant. It must have the proper mixture of elements—neither too much clay nor too much sand.
- Create a proper balance—neither too acid nor too alkaline.
- Cultivate deeply before planting, allowing the soil to breathe.
- Soil should be loose and rich in nutrients.

*Southern Living* magazine customizes their garden section for different areas of the country, enabling gardeners to know how to work with their particular garden needs, those related to their area of the country. The magazine also carries general garden articles, like the one I found about the beauty bush. I took a photo from *Southern Living* to the nursery in my area, in search of an awesome plant called a beauty bush (*Kolkwitzia amabilis*), only to be told it does not grow in North Florida! This plant is described as a bush adorned with small, cascading, trumpet-shaped flowers. I thought I had to have this cascading bush in my small garden—but it was not suited to the soil!

Do you see the point? That bush would never grow in North Florida soil. No wonder Creator God gave individual gifts through the Holy Spirit. He knows the soil of our hearts. I must not try to get my gifts into the soil of my mentee. Rather, together, we must discover her gifts and the soil of her heart. Together, we must work to create the proper balance in the soil of her life so that her gifts will grow. Mentoring requires deep cultivation in friendship to earn trust and the right to mentor.

## Removing the Obstacles

Stones and other obstacles prevent cultivation of the soil. Nothing will stop a tiller quicker than hitting a large stone. The obstacles must be removed before you can work the soil.

Remove the obstacles to friendship. From your own life, remove judgment, condemnation, pride, and self-righteousness. Help your mentee see that doubt, lack of trust, and self-condemnation are obstacles to your relationship that must be removed.

## Adding Elements

Soil that contains too much clay will hold too much water and will be so compact that the plants' roots won't be able to breathe. Nearly everything you plant in such soil will rot. A good gardener will add organic matter and a little sand, enriching the soil and creating breathing room.

Soil that contains too much sand won't hold water and is nutrient poor. Many plants will wither and die in such soil. It will likely need improvement every year.

The soil of a mentee's life may fall into one of three basic categories. One, it may be rich in nutrients and organic matter. Turn the soil and add more nutrients. Provide a little encouragement and direction.

Two, it may contain too much clay and not be getting enough air. This mentee may be full of potential, but circumstances are choking out the possibilities for her. She may lack education and self-confidence. On top of encouragement and direction, you may need to help her get beyond the circumstances that hold her back. This doesn't mean you should try to solve her problems, but help her find her own solutions. If, for example, she needs money to go to school, draw her attention to the many different options such as grants and scholarships. Help to choose the option that best fits her needs, and then encourage her as she does the work. Build self-confidence.

Three, it may be sandy and contain little or no nutrients. Such a mentee may have been neglected or abused. Her needs run deep. Whatever the circumstances, she lacks what it takes to grow. You may be able to help in some areas of her life; but you will need to recognize your limits and know when to refer her to others for more help. Alone, you won't be able to supply all of her needs, but you can help create a nurturing and growing environment with your love and support.

## Achieving Balance

Gardeners test the soil of their gardens for acidity and alkalinity. Then they will add lime or sulfur to create balance.

Your mentee will need help in creating balance in her life. The gung ho woman who always takes on more than she can handle; the timid woman who is afraid to try anything new— you can help them by talking through what is important to them, by helping them set goals or limits.

## Creating Breathing Room

The topsoil in your garden must be loose so the plants won't suffocate. A mentor encourages and teaches, but doesn't hover.

Jane says, "I wasn't looking for another mother. But Suzanne's relationship [with me] is that of very special friends. I value her counsel. I know she won't tell others what we talk about. She doesn't jump on me. Rather she says, 'What do you think of this?' She doesn't preach. She guides."

One of the definitions of mentor is *wise guide*. Guide your mentee toward making good decisions instead of telling her what her decision should be.

An important part of wise guiding is confidentiality. Jane could breathe around Suzanne because she knew she could trust Suzanne not to share her secrets with others. You must respect confidentiality in a mentoring relationship. Otherwise, your mentee's trust in you will be shattered and the relationship will die.

## Working the Soil

1. Remove the obstacles to friendship such as judgment, condemnation, pride, and self-righteousness on your part.
2. Help your mentee see that doubt, lack of trust, and self-condemnation are obstacles to your relationship that must be removed.
3. Add the following elements as needed: encouragement, direction, self-confidence, problem-solving skills, and an environment of love and support.
4. Help your mentee achieve balance in her life through priority and goal setting.
5. Provide guidance instead of judgment and instruction.
6. Maintain confidentiality at all times.
7. Deal with every mentee as a unique and gifted individual.

## Adding Nutrients

In working with my garden, I have also learned that different plants need different nutrients to grow. So does the garden heart of the mentee. Consider the mentee's needs as she enters into this friendship. Every mentor/mentee relationship will be different.

## Proper Tools

Martha Stewart advises the gardener to buy good tools and take care of them. If you do this, good tools will last a long time. Many times I have watched my father, at the end of his gardening day, painstakingly clean his garden tools. He did not come from the throwaway generation. He still uses some of his tools from years ago. When he finishes cleaning, each tool has its place, neatly hung in the basement or toolshed. Woe be to you if you used a tool and did not clean it to his satisfaction, or did not put it back. Why, it would make one give up gardening all together!

Bob and I have an almost-adopted son-in-the-ministry who, to our delight, is our minister of music. Not only is he a fine musician, he is a craftsman who can fix anything—and I mean *anything*. As I watched him put together the shelves and cabinets for our garage, I was amazed. One day I figured it out.

"It's in the tools, isn't it, Paul?" I asked. He smiled knowingly.

Many times I've tackled a project without the proper tools and ended up making a mess. It's one thing to use the wrong tools with a bookcase, even another with a garden where you can start over—but with a life, such a mistake could be costly.

Remember that Song of Solomon 1:3a (NASB) says, "Your oils have a pleasing fragrance, Your name is like purified oil."

Purified oil is oil which has been emptied from one vessel to another. As we empty ourselves first before God and then into each other in this purifying process, the fragrance of Christ will permeate our world. The word picture of this passage is powerful—your name, the Scripture says, is purified in such a way that the fragrance of Christ is being poured out . . . poured out into another . . . releasing the fragrance of Christ. Yes!!! Yes!!!

Women have unprecedented opportunity to work with their God-given tools in the soil of the hearts and lives of other women. Locate the garden. Plan the garden. Make the garden bed, and work with good tools as you make eternal investment in the lives of women.

Remember, garden soil takes work. Mentoring will not always be easy, but we live in a day and time when mentoring is desperately needed. Are you willing to work in someone's garden as a mentor? to be an inspiration? to help them learn to bear fruit? Then, you must work in the garden soil of their lives to develop friendship, self-confidence, balance, and trust, using the tools of faith in and reliance on God, wisdom, truth in action, a listening and nonjudging heart, the will to keep trying, and joy in the success of others. Garden soil takes work!

## The Proper Tools

- faith in God
- reliance on God
- wisdom from God
- truth in action for God
- grace and mercy of God
- ears to listen to them for God
- perseverance, strength, and joy from God

# VI

## *Sowing the Seeds*

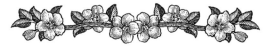

The movie adaptation of *The Secret Garden* took some liberties with scenes and script, but some of its words and scenes are profound! At the close of the movie, Master Colin is reunited with his estranged father, the garden has been restored in beauty by Mary and Dickon, and life at the Misselthwaite Manor is overflowing in joy. Mary, watching Colin and his father embrace, is overwhelmed with sadness and contentment, experiencing the garden of hope she planted in Colin, while at the same time embracing hope herself. She says, "If you look in just the right way, you'll see the whole world is a garden."

What awesome insight! She is right, you know. It is a matter of looking at your world . . . seeing the things that need *turning around* and adjusting your glasses so you, too, can see the world in need of God's love through the intentional touch of a mentoring life.

In the beginning of the movie, as Mary moves into the manor, she discovers there is a secret garden. She begins to look for the key to the gate. Having made friends with the old gardener, she asks about the garden and is told the bird knows the way. In conversation with the little bird, she asks, "If you know the way, show me."

I believe young women today are asking . . . no, shouting, "If you know the way, show me!" Mentoring is showing someone the way to the secret garden in their life, opening their eyes to the world of possibilities by planting seeds.

### Open Their Eyes to the Possibilities

I asked one of my former students, Becky Hartzog, to share a life-changing experience with me. These are her words:

> As a college junior I was given an opportunity unlike any I had ever experienced. Selected to be a part of a mission team from Samford University, I

joined 18 other students in a three-week study of the
inner city. Under the leadership of our campus minister,
Esther Burroughs, we then headed for New York City to
do a mission project. Assigned the task of renovating an
old storefront into a day-care center for the children of
an East Manhattan neighborhood, our team of excited,
naive, and invincible college students set about tearing
the place apart!

While Graffiti Center was not completely finished
when we held the grand opening, it had undergone a
tremendous transformation. We learned that mission
work is never finished. We left, knowing another BSU
group would follow and build on what we had started.

The greatest changes that took place that week took
place in the lives of the students who participated in the
project. Of the 19 who went to New York City, 13
became involved in Christian ministry or missions after
college graduation.

As a campus minister, I am one of the 13. New York
City opened my eyes to a whole new world. The
people I met gave me a new concept of God's love and
*seeing with the heart.* Because of that experience during
my college days, mission trips have become a priority in
my ministry with college students, as well as with youth
groups in the churches where I have served.

One of the highlights of being a
campus minister is seeing students get
excited about the possibilities of ministry
and missions through such a trip. It always
takes me back to 1975, to a campus
minister who had faith in me, and to an
experience that continues to have a major
impact on my life—as well as on the lives
of those students with whom I work.

What a bouquet of
Flowering Almond,
*hope,* you are! What a
fragrance you must be
to God! Thank you,
Becky Hartzog.

You can help open up a world of possibilities in the life of your mentee through
the seeds you plant—the ideas, the values,
the direction, the hope. Or, if you are searching for the key to a
beautiful garden life, you can find these same ideas, values,
direction, and hope through the loving guidance of a mentor.

Just as God guided you to a mentee, or guided a mentee to you, God will guide you in knowing which seeds to plant.

## Mentors Must Be Planted

"And I will appoint a place for My people Israel, and will plant them, that they may dwell in their own place and be moved no more; neither shall the wicked waste them anymore" (1 Chron. 17:9 NASB).

In this passage, the seed represents the people of God. God is the Sower and He plants us where He wants us to be. God reminds David that He walked with His people and gave them a name like the great ones in the earth. God is our *dwelling place*, so only our address changes in life—not the dwelling place.

I spent days searching God's Word for references regarding planting, seeds, harvesting, and fruit. It was a wonderful journey for me to see again God's plan for His people, Israel. The Master Gardener *planted* them with a purpose—to show that He was their God.

Warren W. Weirsbe's *Expository Outlines on the Old Testament* says, "Isaiah shows us Israel was Jehovah's servant in that the nation was used of God to bring the Word and the Savior to the world. However, Israel was a disobedient servant that had to be chastened. Jesus Christ is the true Servant of Jehovah who died for the world and perfectly did His Father's will."

That led me to *Webster's* dictionary: "Plant: a sprout put in the ground to grow: to settle: to establish." God meant to plant, to grow, to settle, to establish His Kingdom through Israel.

In John 15:1 (NASB), Jesus said, "I am the true vine, and My Father is the vinedresser." Everything you need to know about vinedressing and planting, God knows. Jesus is the true Vine, deeply rooted in the soil of God's redemptive plan, and we are the branches, which bear fruit in His vineyard.

I was speaking at a women's retreat in Fort Worth, Texas, and heard a beautiful young woman sing Steven Curtis Chapman's song, "Show Yourselves to Be." I recall the text was right out of John 15: "They will know that you are Mine, like the branches of the vine, if you show yourselves to be following Me."[1]

Can't you just imagine Jesus walking through the gardens, reaching up and getting a cluster of grapes from the vine as He begins the lesson of John 15? Watch Him gently kick a clod of dirt beneath the vine as He gives illustrations that the people of

Israel understand. He tells them that He is the true Vine; and only through being connected to the Vine, only through faith in Christ, do we have life.

Every plant has to be rooted in soil to live. Every mentor has to be rooted in the Vine to live and to mentor. Plant yourself in Christ and God will guide you in planting your life in another.

## Sowing Directly Into the Soil

Seeds that are sown directly into the soil may or may not live, and they flower later than those sown in controlled conditions. Direct-sown seeds are subject to the whims of nature—so many things can happen before they have a chance to take root. They may be scorched by drought, washed away by floods, or eaten by birds. Those that do survive will flower later in the season because the gardener had to wait to sow them.

The same could be said about seeds that are sown directly into the soil of a human life. Much of the seed that is tossed at human beings never takes root because it isn't nurtured until it can take root and grow strong.

## Transplanting

Eight weeks passed after the landscaping company promised they would be here to put in the rock wall which would give definition and form to my English garden. I missed the time to plant bulbs. Oh, don't worry! I still had my garden, because I plant everything in pots initially. I meant to do that anyway for the annuals. It was the perennials that I didn't get in the ground in time that season.

The wonderful thing to remember about gardening is that seasons always follow seasons. It is a cycle that happens every year. Much gardening is done through the transplanting process. My garden began a long time ago because someone somewhere put tiny seeds in a small container. When they were just an inch or so in height, the seeds were thinned out and transplanted into a garden bed or larger containers, ready to be sent to nurseries or garden shops.

The process of transplanting increases a seed's chance of survival. It can be nurtured and cared for in a controlled environment until the proper season for planting comes back around. Most mentoring is done through the process of transplanting. Seeds are planted in small containers in the soil of a human life.

They are nurtured and cared for until they are strong. When the proper season for their growth rolls around, the seedlings are transplanted into the larger garden and allowed to spread and grow—blossoming for the world to see.

As a young woman helped her mother thin and transplant some garden flowers, she asked this longtime gardener, "Doesn't this hurt them?"

The mother replied, "Oh no, this only makes their roots grow deep and strong."

That's what happens in our lives when we choose to transplant our love, knowledge, life experience, and caring heart into someone else's life. The roots grow strong, equipping us to work in the soil of someone's life.

Another aspect of transplanting is the process of thinning and replanting. Seeds of faith require thinning and transplanting, and in the process of transplanting, your faith will grow deeper and stronger. From the work of God in the mentor's life of abiding, she pours and empties herself into another. It is in this refining process, pouring the fragrant oil from one vessel to another, that the mentoring takes place and the fragrance is released.

As you mentor, as you transplant skills and values, hopes and dreams, remember you are working with a life, not with a flower that is here today and gone tomorrow. As you plant seeds, your place is that of a fieldworker in God's harvest. We must never forget it is His field and His seed—and it is God Who will give the harvest!

## Seeds of Faith
### • The Word of God

"Listen carefully: Unless a grain of wheat is buried in the ground, dead to the world, it is never any more than a grain of wheat. But if it is buried, it sprouts and reproduces itself many times over. In the same way, anyone who holds on to life just as it is destroys that life. But if you let it go, reckless in your love, you'll have it forever, real and eternal" (John 12:24–25 *The Message*).

Jesus knows about seeds. He referred to Himself as the real Vine and His Father as the Farmer. Jesus also knows about the human heart. It is like soil, and soil has tremendous potential. If the Word of God is seed and the heart is soil, then God's Word is made for the heart.

The strongest mentoring will come out of a heart that has died to self and celebrates living as a new creation compelled to make an eternal difference. As a mentor, ask God to increase your desire for His Word, which is the seed. When it is planted in your heart and its truth rooted in your life, it brings forth new life.

Your mentee may or may not be a Christian. If your mentee is a Christian, help her to learn the personal discipline it takes to study the Word of God and to develop a thirst for God. Plant the seed words of Colossians 2:6–7 (NASB) in her heart: "As you therefore have received Christ Jesus the Lord, so walk in Him, having been firmly rooted and now being built up in Him and established in your faith, just as you were instructed, and over-flowing with gratitude."

Place Ephesians 3:17–19 (NASB) deep in the heart of your mentee: "So that Christ may dwell in your hearts through faith; and that you, being rooted and grounded in love, may be able to comprehend with all the saints what is the breadth and length and height and depth, and to know the love of Christ which sur-passes knowledge, that you may be filled up to all the fulness of God."

If your mentee is not a Christian, pray for opportunities to live out your faith before her, creating in her a hunger to know the source of your faith. Remember that the Scripture says, "But a natural man does not accept the things of the Spirit of God; for they are foolishness to him, and he cannot understand them" (1 Cor. 2:14*a* NASB). Share your faith carefully and prayerfully, so that you don't turn her away from God before she has a chance to see God in you.

### • **Prayer**

One of Huber Drumwright's memories from his childhood was a large bed of old-fashioned violets in the yard of his grandparents' home. At some point, his mother transplanted some of those flowers into their own yard. Huber's wife, Minette, continues the story:

> As a bride and groom, Huber and I *borrowed* from his parents' home and transplanted the descendant vio-lets to our little parsonage in Allen, Texas. We moved to Dallas and then to Fort Worth, each time taking with us some of the violets that had originated in his grand-mother's flower beds.

Our daughters, Meme and Debra, recall that from their earliest memories, our home had a prolific border of violets all the way across the front of our house.

When we moved to Little Rock, Arkansas, of course, we moved the family violets with us! Once again, they multiplied well at our new home.

After Huber's death in late 1981, I remained in Little Rock for nearly a year before moving to Richmond. Debra and Max married one month prior to my move and they took transplants of the violets with them from Little Rock to their little home in Fort Worth. I did not attempt to take any of the violets to Richmond, depending on my kids to preserve the family tradition 'till I returned to Texas!

Recently, in my move back to Fort Worth, I arrived to find Debra and Max bordering one of my new flower beds with the descendant family violets, transplanted once again—this time from their home to mine. Meme and H. W. have them in their yard in Austin, also. This means that my three grandchildren are growing up with violets whose floral ancestors came from their great, great grandparents' home.

Thank you, Minette Drumwright, my dear sister in Christ, for your letter. I give violets to you, of course, as a sweet bouquet: Rural, *happiness*; Yellow, *faithfulness*; Blue, *watchfulness*; Dame, *sweet modesty.* What a fragrant aroma!

Minette has been involved in the transplanting of violets; yet, an even sweeter aroma caresses those in whom she has transplanted a faith in the power of prayer. Many generations will breathe in the sweetness of faith in a God Who works through prayer because of the thousands of lives affected by one woman's belief in prayer—prayer that has touched and continues to touch lives around the world for Christ. Plant the seeds of faith in God Who works through prayer in your mentee.

Monte Clendinning has served God in many different ways and in many different places. Monte writes about one woman who planted seeds of prayer in her life:

Dr. Floy Barnard, affectionately known as Miss B, was my mentor. She was the Dean of Women while I was a student at Southwestern Baptist Theological Seminary, Fort Worth, Texas. My senior year, I had the privilege of being her assistant as I served as president of the dorm. I learned from her how to deepen my prayer life. Each night at 10:00, she led the dorm residents in a prayer circle. When Miss B prayed, I felt as if I were lifted into the very presence of the Father. We experienced many answers to prayer throughout those years in the circle.

Can't you just breathe in the fragrance of the relationship between the dean and her dorm prayer circle?

Monte was one of my mentors. When Monte is praying, I feel the very presence of God. Everyone present in the room senses the intimacy of her relationship with her Heavenly Father.

Monte has been the fragrance of God on the missions field, in her local church in women's work, and on a seminary campus in the World Mission Center. Recently, Monte retired; yet she and her husband, Pat, are overseas again, mentoring and planting their lives in missionaries—releasing the fragrance of Christ.

Blue Violets, *faithfulness,* to Pat and Monte

If your mentee is not a Christian, fill your days with prayer for her. In teaching the Christian mentee about prayer, show her how to read the Bible expectantly, asking God for a verse over which to pray in life situations. Show her how to pray through your example. Pray with her and for her.

### • Ministry and Missions

July 19, 1996, the opening ceremonies of the 100th Olympiad were held in Atlanta, Georgia. It was a great event, as it always is. Many churches sent representatives to the Olympics, representatives who transplanted their lives from one state to a temporary state, for the purpose of *ministry*—joining with the thousands of Olympic athletes. I'm proud that thousands of Christians, from all denominations, joined in the *transplanting* of lives in Atlanta that summer. Because their lives were rooted deep in Christian love, these volunteers were able to give of themselves and transplant the seeds of God's love as they shared hospitality in a cup of cold water or ministered through a gospel tract, sun lotion, and their own living letter, representing Christ Jesus.

Plant in your mentee seeds of concern for the people she meets every day. Instill courage to reach out.

As a young pastor's wife, my friend Stuart Calvert had some bad experiences with missions groups during their time at seminary. They had a new church and a new chance at being involved in missions; but Stuart really wasn't thrilled about the prospect of another missions group.

"Mrs. Haggard cultivated my friendship. She called to welcome me, sent notes, and stopped by the house occasionally. Mrs. Haggard was loving and kind," Stuart said.

Mrs. Haggard and others persisted, drawing Stuart in, encouraging her to participate, giving her responsibility. One day Mrs. Haggard invited Stuart to go to a meeting with her at Camp Garaywa. "I want you to listen to Miss Edwina Robinson. She can inspire you," Mrs. Haggard said.

When Stuart opened the door, Miss Ed was in mid-sentence.

"Immediately, I was enthralled by her rapid staccato delivery. She had a command of the English language that I will go to the grave envying. I was overwhelmed with her mastery of facts, not only about Mississippi but about the whole world. What happened that

Mrs. Haggard's bouquet would be a huge basket of White Dittany, *passion*. I don't know what Dittany looks like, but I do know what passion for missions looks like in a woman's heart! Think of the fragrant offering Mrs. Haggard laid at the feet of Christ when she chose to mentor Stuart Calvert, who in turn mentors multitudes through her writings, and hundreds more through her ministry.

day? When I drove into Garaywa, I pictured the world as a dark globe—suspended somewhere out there. When I drove out of Garaywa, the world was not suspended somewhere out there—it was in my heart.

"Mrs. Haggard used her leadership gift to mentor me. She cared about an ignorant pastor's wife. In love, she trained me. Since meeting Mrs. Haggard when I was 24, every opportunity the Lord gives me is a direct result of her influential mentoring."

Stuart is an active woman on mission for God today. Stuart's concerns, prayers, and actions are global because one woman

My bouquet to Stuart Calvert would be a vase of Pansies, meaning *thoughts*, because her thoughts have deeply touched my life . . . in her writings, in prayers on my behalf, and in her friendship in my life.

took the time to help her see the world as God sees it.

Plant seeds of missions-mindedness in your mentee. Plant a view of a world in need of Christ and inspire her to meet that need. Plant tears and compassion for those who are lost and hurting.

## Roots of Character

A friend of mine had a small garden area which contained little but weeds and violets. Lori's garden scheme didn't include violets. Digging up the violets was difficult because their roots run deep and cling tightly to the soil. But she finished digging them up and planted other flowers in their place—at least she thought she had dug them all up!

Barely a week had passed before new violets began to spring up in spots that weren't even close to where the original plants had been! She dug those up, only to have others spring up later. You see, violets extend themselves and multiply through root stems that they send underground. They are nearly impossible to eliminate once they have taken root.

Violets spread, and so do character traits. Character traits planted in your life will send out root stems into the lives around you. Once these character traits take root in the life of your mentee, others will be hard pressed to uproot them. Their roots will grow strong and deep.

### Roots of Character

1. What character traits have spread into your life from another?
2. What character traits are strong enough in your life to send out root stems into the life of your mentee?
3. What character traits need to be planted in your life so that you can pass them along to another?

I was given a gift by a young couple and was so delighted with the purpose. The *Do Unto Others Plate²* is a practical tool to help you teach your children how to commit the Golden Rule to memory. The concept of the plate is simple. Any family member can nominate another person to receive the award. The only qualifier is that the recipient must have exhibited behavior that was first thoughtful of others. The parents award the plate at the family mealtime. The *Do Unto Others Plate* is designed to become a family tradition as well as a cherished heirloom, passed from one generation to the next. It will teach little children how to have big hearts, while reminding them that actions speak louder than words.

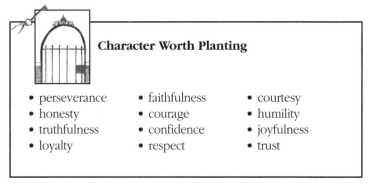

### Character Worth Planting

* perseverance
* honesty
* truthfulness
* loyalty

* faithfulness
* courage
* confidence
* respect

* courtesy
* humility
* joyfulness
* trust

Beverly D. Sutton's mother mentored her, planting the seeds of belief in her as a child of God and giving her perseverance. Beverly, now a professor of pediatrics nursing, teaches and mentors students and delights in being told things like every one of the students she tutored has passed the state board exams!

Transplanting what she was taught by her mother, she is inspired as she observes, "Inner-city children in our after-school program display courtesy and respect for each other." She is transplanting life.

Roots of perseverance and faith, of courtesy and respect, spread from Beverly's mother to Beverly, and from Beverly to the students she mentors.

## Seeds of Hope, Inspiration, and Love

I call these the seeds of "you can do it," "pick a dream, any dream," and "even if you can't do this, you are a wonderful person. Let's go discover what you can do better than anyone else!"

Nancy Beach, administrative assistant at Willow Creek Community Church in Chicago, said that Bill Hybels was at one time her youth group leader. In her, he "planted the seeds of excellence and a passion for harnessing the arts for ministry."

Nancy later served as a teaching assistant to Em Griffin, a professor of communications at Wheaton College. She said, "He taught me a leadership style that cares for the whole person, including interpersonal communication skills and group dynamics."

When asked about her own mentoring style, she replied, "The idea is not to clone yourself, but to engage your energy, experience, and God-given wisdom toward the development of another woman . . . freeing her to reach her unique potential which may look very much different from your own." Nancy delights in seeing those whom she has mentored "take off in their confidence, exceed my own abilities, and lead in their own unique style."

Plant hope in your mentees by believing in them and their ability to achieve great things. Inspire them to dream good and growing dreams. And above all else, love them into becoming the unique, gifted, and confident women God created them to be. Love them through self-doubt, through failure, through hard times and good times.

## Praying for the Harvest

Jesus controls the harvest. In another story about the Kingdom of God, the disciples asked Jesus to explain the wheat and the tares. He answered with these words in Matthew 13:37*b*-39 (NASB): "The one who sows the good seed is the Son of Man, and the field is the world; and as for the good seed, these are the sons of the kingdom; and the tares are the sons of the evil one; and the enemy who sowed them is the devil, and the harvest is the end of the age; and the reapers are angels."

Surely, Jesus was saying to His followers: If you let Me plant you in My field, you will touch the world.

As mentors—women with a mission, mothers, sisters, friends—as we guide others we must remember that this is His field, not ours. In today's world, Christians of all denominations must hold hands as field workers, dying to our agendas, praying for reconciliation among believers, and embracing each other as Kingdom citizens, in humility at the privilege of serving the owner the field. We must remember that the harvest comes at the end of the age, not at the end of a program, the mentoring relationship, a successful retreat, or a church service.

Wiersbe said he could remember how in times past, when pastors finished their sermons at the end of a service, they did not go to the back of the church to greet the members. Instead, they went back to their studies, got on their knees, and prayed to the Lord of the harvest to bring forth a harvest from the seed that had just been planted.

*Wow!* I sat in the Samford University chapel, remembering my own precious father, knowing that was exactly what he did following his sermons. I never thought about seeing him at the back door greeting the people. He was back in his study begging God for a harvest!

What if all women at the close of a mentoring session or the end of a women's meeting/retreat, would go back to their rooms and kneel before God, asking Him for a harvest from the seeds that were just planted? That would, indeed, turn things around!

### Planting Seeds

In the life of your mentee . . .

- transplant faith that will lead her to new life in Christ or cause her roots to sink deeper in Christ.

- send out root stems of character that will strengthen her against the hard times and enable her to truly enjoy the good times.

- plant seeds of hope that will help her to see what is good in her, seeds of inspiration that enable her to see what she can be, and seeds of love that will envelop and comfort her in the bad times and enable her to blossom in fragrant beauty always!

# Part Three
# Nurturing Growth

# VII
## Just the Right Light

Sunlight is one of the most important factors in gardening. Different types of plants must be positioned differently to ensure that they receive just the right sunlight.

The same can be said of mentoring. Mentees must be positioned to receive just the right amount of Sonlight. Your relationship with Christ is key to your ability to reflect Sonlight on the non-Christian mentee, as well as to position the Christian to receive the Sonlight.

Suzanne has a special concern for young mothers with small children, many with non-Christian husbands. She has also faced those same challenges. Though her husband has now come to know Christ, and her own children are grown, she still continues to encourage women with small children. She chooses to serve on the child-care committee of her church so she can stay in touch with these young mothers and encourage them.

Ruth had this to say about Suzanne: "One day, I was so low. I was in my third pregnancy and my husband had just been laid off work again. Suzanne came over and we just talked. Her spiritual perspective gave me the desire to keep going."

Suzanne worked to position Ruth in the light of Christ by helping her see her situation from a different perspective.

A woman with *life experience* and *spiritual perspective* can look on the situation and see what those on the inside cannot. She can share through Christ's eyes, so that Christ's vision can be shared. She invests the soil of her life experiences in someone else, enriching the life; she positions what she is planting life so that it can receive the Sonlight and grow strong.

Second Corinthians 9:10–11, from *The Message*, says this: "This most generous God who gives seed to the farmer that becomes bread for your meals is more than extravagant with you. He gives you something you can then give away, which grows into full-formed lives, robust in God, wealthy in every way, so that you can be generous in every way, producing with us great praise to God."

One year, Bob and I were in Switzerland, attending the International Church Music Festival. We found ourselves seated at a table with Roger and Diane McMurrin. In our table conversation, these new friends told us of a very unique journey the Lord had allowed them to make in recent years.

Roger and Diane took a choir to Kiev, Ukraine, on a missions trip, and the Lord spoke to them. They felt the strong call of God to return to this area.

After returning home, Roger resigned from a very large, prestigious church in South Florida. They sold their home, cashed in their retirement, and moved to Kiev to begin a new ministry.

Roger is an excellent choral conductor/teacher, and he began a professional choir and orchestra. Every six weeks, they performed major religious works, most of which had never been heard in the Ukraine. Many were hymns that had not been sung in the churches in decades. Roger and Diane have now started a new church, which Roger is co-pastoring with a national pastor.

In disbelief, you might ask, *Why?* Why would Roger and Diane give up so much to move halfway around the world and start all over in ministry? For position in the Sonlight! Roger and Diane were simply following the Son and looking for ways to position new lives in the Sonlight.

## Fruit That Remains

What faith Roger and Diane have in the Vinedresser, Who said in John 15:16 (NASB), "You did not choose Me, but I chose you . . . that you should go and bear fruit, and that your fruit should remain, that whatever you ask of the Father in My name, He may give to you."

What a concept! Chosen to live in such a way that what you do remains. That, my precious sisters, is a good definition of mentoring.

I heard Jean Shepherd, a Wycliffe Bible translator, comment during a student missions conference, "I want to do something with my life that will last forever and will go on without me."

Dig deep into the soil of your life. What nutrients do you find? Where is your connection? What are you planting that will remain long after you are gone? Is it positioned in the Son of God? Connected to the true Vine? Trust the Vinedresser.

Live by His instruction in John 15:16 (NASB): "That whatever you ask of the Father in My name, He may give to you."

## The Harvest Belongs to God

I heard a story several years ago of Mother Teresa, when she was speaking at a Washington, DC, press conference. Describing her ministry, she said she is called to the *poorest of the poor*. Drawn to the Spirit of God in this little woman after she spoke, people stood around her, not wanting to leave, wanting only to be in her presence.

A government official was overheard to ask her: "One of the things you said tonight I just don't understand. You told us that as you minister to these dying people, over half of them literally die in the arms of the sisters in your order. You have a failure statistic of 50 percent. How do you deal with that kind of failure?"

Mother Teresa, dressed in muslin garb held together with safety pins, straightened to all of her 4-foot, 11-inch height. Then looking up at him, she said, "Oh sir . . . My God has never called me to be successful . . . only faithful."

Her ministry has impacted the world. Here is one woman who is willing to work in the dirty soil of the lives of the poor, showing a world how to be *rich*. May the fragrance of her garden help you see a Master Who is still inviting us to leave everything and trust and follow Him, that His fruit will remain in you.

Position yourself and your mentee in the Sonlight of God and trust God for a harvest that will remain.

## Sonlight

1. The most important aspect of Christian mentoring is the amount of Sonlight received. Mentors and mentees alike must receive the full light of the Son of God to bear fruit.

2. God gives the harvest. If both mentor and mentee remain in the Son, God will cause them to bear fruit that will remain, to live lives with eternal significance.

# VIII
## *When to Water and Fertilize*

"It's not the one who plants or the one who waters who is at the center of this process but God, who makes things grow. You happen to be God's field in which we are working" (1 Cor. 3:7, 9 *The Message*).

Mentors *enhance* growth in the lives of others. When a gardener plants seeds in a garden, the work has really just begun.

We had driven all the way from Abilene, Texas, to Birmingham, Alabama, in two cars, with two small children, so Bob could begin his new position as composer-in-residence on the music faculty of Samford University. We were tired as we drove onto the street of our home on that hot August afternoon. The house had just been completed, which meant there was no grass!

Imagine our great surprise as we turned into our driveway to discover Claude Rhea, dean of the Samford University School of Music, and his two sons, Claude III and Randy, on their knees, sodding our front yard! We were overwhelmed and grateful.

When we left that wonderful home ten years later, the yard was a picture of beauty. It was there I planted my first daisies. I learned in those years that yards and gardens require constant care: feeding, watering, weeding, and pruning.

You've selected the garden site, made plans, worked the soil, and planted seeds in the right light. It won't be long now before you begin to see sprouts of new life. You'll transplant these seedlings into large pots, and eventually into the garden, where they'll root and grow rapidly. But your work as a gardener does not end here! There is much to be done before your plants will flower and bear fruit.

### Nourishment from the Vine
Could the lesson of John 15 be that God, in Jesus Christ, means for us to trust Him and not trust ourselves? If we understand the

vine and branch connection, we realize we must trust God, the Vinedresser, to do for and through us what we cannot do for ourselves. His chosen people, Israel, did not follow obediently. They kept forgetting Jehovah God and trusting themselves. Yet, Jehovah so loved His creation that He sent another message— The Message—Jesus Christ.

Isaiah gives a rich, prophetic picture of Jesus Christ. The word *Isaiah* means *the salvation of Jehovah.* Describing Jesus, Isaiah 53:2*a* (NASB) says, "For He grew up before Him like a tender shoot, And like a root out of parched ground; He has no stately form or majesty That we should look upon Him." Isaiah pictures the nation of Israel as a tree cut down; the stump remains and a new shoot will grow from it. Surely you have seen that happen in your garden. A tree stump has a branch growing from it, continuing life from the tree. Warren W. Wiersbe, in his *Expository Outlines on the Old Testament,* says, "The words, 'tender plant' literally mean 'little bush,' such as would spring from a low branch." What a great word picture! The Creator of the universe, Sculptor of the Swiss Alps, Maker of the Canadian Rockies, Artist of the Grand Canyon, Designer of Victoria Falls, and the Watercolor Painter of the Great Barrier Reef—is presented to us as a little bush, a tender plant! For a moment, stoop down with Isaiah to see the tender plant on a low branch—showing us the gentle love of God with small beginnings, all about saving and resurrecting power, the life-changing, world-changing, eternity-changing, *little branch.* Jeremiah 33:15 refers to Jesus as *the righteous Branch.*

In Isaiah 6:1, 3, we see the nation chopped down as a tree, with a stump remaining. Then we see Christ coming from this stump to save His people in Isaiah 11:1, and we are invited, in John 15, to be connected to that life-giving Branch.

Isaiah 60:21 (NASB) tells us, "Then all your people will be righteous; They will possess the land forever, The branch of My planting, The work of My hands, That I may be glorified." See the connection between *that I may be glorified* and *fruit that remains?* When the vine and the branch abide in each other, the fruit remains, and the Father is glorified. *Yes! Yes!* What other challenge do we need to become obedient as women of God, grafted into the Vine, His life flowing through ours, planting in the soil of another, to be put in the ground to grow.

Jesus Christ is *the branch,* the legal descendant of David, *rooted* in Judah, and Himself, a Jew. The Hebrew word *netzer* (branch) ties in with the name given to Jesus in Matthew 2:23: *the Nazarene*. They said about Him: "Can anything good come out of Nazareth?" We respond: "Yes! Our salvation came from Jesus, the Nazarene!"

Jeremiah 32:40*a*–41*b* (NASB) says, "And I will make an everlasting covenant with them. . . I will faithfully plant them in this land with all My heart and with all My soul." He, Jehovah God, through Jesus, the Vine, chooses to plant in us—His people—to cultivate love in relationships and to bear fruit in the Kingdom.

It is only out of the Vine that we are able to produce fruit. Any plant that loses its connection from the branch is no longer receiving sustaining life nutrients and will soon wither and die. Any believer who is not abiding in the Father, the Vinedresser, and making a home within the Father, and letting the Father make His home in that believer, has no way to receive the life-giving nutrients. Like the vine, that believer withers and dies.

Remember, I told you how I planned my garden so that I could see it from every room in my house? The garden began to take shape in late June! It now brings me great pleasure to be able to see it as I walk through the rooms of our home. Surely the Father would have us look at Him in the same way. No matter what room of life we are in at the moment, and no matter what circumstances we are facing, if we keep a focused view of His deep and abiding presence in our lives, His work will continue in the soil of our hearts. Isn't that a comforting thought?

As I was visiting one morning with our landscape contractor, I asked him about our weeping willow. It had green branches up to about six feet, but the top seemed dead and bare. I ask him if it was dead or dying. "Oh, no!" he answered. "The branches closest to the roots always come to life first."

Wow! What a great spiritual truth! Those believers who are closest to the Root—Jesus—will come to life first . . . because they are closest to the nourishment of the Vine!

Abiding is not a casual relationship. Abiding is a very distinct, conscious relationship, a voluntary union of two wills. Jesus invites us to live life with Him on a deep level. In John 15:4*a* (NASB), Jesus extends this invitation: "Abide in Me, and I in you." No wonder the Father says that apart from Him we cannot bear fruit. Apart from Him, we will do nothing that impacts eternity. *Webster's* defines abiding this way: "To remain with someone, to reside with, to stand fast, and to submit to someone." Abiding is to make a home within.

Dag Hammarskjöld, the general secretary to the United Nations from 1953 to 1961, said, "Abiding is God's marriage with the soul."

Thomas Merton said, "Abiding is a consciousness of our union with God, it is a reminder of our complete dependence on Him for all of the vital acts of our spiritual life, and His constant loving presence in the very depth of our soul."

I would add:

- *Abiding* is our connection with God.
- *Abiding* is our constant surrendering in this relationship.
- *Abiding* is living in Christ and Christ living through our lives.
- *Abiding* is learning the secret of the mystery of Christ.

Anna Esther, our first granddaughter, sent me a very special gift after I returned from a speaking engagement in Egypt. It was a childlike drawing of Anna and me with the heads so close together that they are connected. It is a good illustration of an abiding relationship! I show the original drawing often when talking about intimacy with God. The con-  cept is that Jesus Christ is living His life through us—overlapping His life with our lives. Abiding is letting Christ do in us what He wants to do, and what we cannot do by ourselves.

It makes me think of the gift my father gave me as I left home in Canada to travel to Mars Hill College in North Carolina. I would be traveling thousands of miles from home, and knew I would not be able to come home for any holidays. As I boarded the bus, my father said, "I want to give you a gift that will last you all year as you are away from home."

He then quoted to me Proverbs 3:5–6 (NASB): "Trust in the Lord with all your heart, And do not lean on your own understanding. In all your ways acknowledge Him, And He will make your paths straight." I've held onto those words time and time again. This Scripture is one of my life verses!

Have you noticed there is a connection between *all your*

*heart* and *all your ways?* You trust with all your heart and He directs all your ways. Abiding is not striving and straining. It is resting, like a baby in its mother's womb. During a normal gestation process, the baby doesn't have to worry about anything, trusting completely in someone other than itself, in this case the mother, the life-giver. The baby gets everything it needs from the mother.

Bob and I know this from personal experience. With our first pregnancy, after the birth of a stillborn son, the doctors said that from conception the fetus did not get enough blood or food necessary to sustain life beyond seven-and-one-half months and therefore could not live any longer. Like a child connected by the life-sustaining umbilical cord, we are bound to our Life-Giver by the cord of love.

As God leads you to mentor someone, lead that person to the Life-Giver and to the promises of God's Word, so she will learn to trust Him more and you less. Help her develop a thirst to study God's Word. Do this by sharing God's Word and how it has directed your path in life. Share out of your own story and relationship with your Heavenly Father.

You and I must keep that branch and vine connection between God, the Father, Who is our source of life, giving everything we need to love and serve Him. The Vine (our Father) has the responsibility to make available for us the power, the love, and the resources we need. The branches (that's us) must stay connected, receiving the power, love, and resources. This connection to our Life-Giver is in the abiding, and out of the abiding comes life poured into another.

In abiding, one must dig deep to:

- determine to grow in Him;
- decide a place to meet Him daily;
- devour His Word, as if a love letter from Him;
- delight His heart with singing;
- depend on and surrender to Him.

Abiders who dig deep find great benefits. They:

- exude grace in stress;
- ensure change from the inside out;
- embrace the promises of God;

- entrust others to Christ;
- experience empowered living.

All of this comes to us because He abides in us as we abide in Him. We will bear fruit, not because we work hard, but because He chooses to abide in and work through us. Bearing fruit means anything in our lives that honors God. It is not just leading people to know Christ. It is anything about our lives that points people to Jesus. It is the attitude in which we live. An attitude is like a shadow. It's what people sense about us, and it speaks louder than words. It is what we are that brings honor to God. Someone said, "True spirituality is the unconscious influence that makes Christ real to others."

Imagine you and I having the ability to change the atmosphere by our presence, or rather by the presence or fragrance of Christ in us. Living in this way brings honor to Christ. The abiding comes out of us in life situations as we show our connection to the branch. It is joy in and through all of life's circumstances. As a mentor, abide in Christ and lead your mentee to do the same. As a mentee, you too must abide in Christ, the source of our spiritual food, to experience growth.

## Drenched in Prayer

A well-watered life is a life drenched in prayer. It is the soul's link with the Father. It is the heart's cry before the Father's throne. It is the altar of praise and adoration before God. You must continue to pour prayer over your mentee.

You might look for a specific verse to pray for and with your mentee as you work together. Share answered prayers with the mentee that will encourage her faith. Tell her part of your life story in which God asked you to die to self in order to bring glory to Himself, and how you prayed through the situation. Many lack a family story that gives tradition and spiritual value to their lives. Be honest in sharing the pain and struggle you have experienced in life, again giving hope because you made it through—and so will she.

If she is a Christian, suggest that she search for a specific verse to pray for a year. And if she has a husband or children, suggest that she select a verse to pray for them for a year. Suggest that she keep a record of her prayertime and let that record show her how God manifests Himself throughout that year.

## Fertilize with Vision and Care

Share your vision. Then help your mentee shape and put words to her own vision, drawing her into ownership of the vision. Think of the impact this could have in the area of missions involvement, lifestyle, parenting, or professional direction!

As you work together, you will get to know your mentee and what is happening in her life.

When you sense a certain weariness or know trouble is brewing, share a hug or a prayer. Call your mentee and see how you can specifically pray for her. Send notes of encouragement. I often tell audiences that I long for an older woman in my daughter's church to call her and ask how she could pray for her on that day—and then follow up the prayer request. Just think of the difference it would make in the life of a woman, her family, and her friends to be mentored in prayer by a woman of God. What an impact it would have on the lives of our children to know that a friend is praying for them specifically! It would also teach our children they can pray for the families of others.

The Emory Gaskins family lives in Fort Worth, Texas. Both parents serve faithfully in ministry, he, as a pastor and she, as the director of work with teenage girls. Cindy shared with me that each night their oldest daughter, Bethany, is allowed to pray for a family member, a friend, and a missionary. For some time, I was the missionary for whom Bethany prayed. What a precious treasure to my life, especially since it had been my joy to mentor Bethany's mother when she was a college student!

*The Message* translation of John 15 refers to Jesus as the Real Vine and His Father as the Farmer. It is out of the intimate relationship with the Real Vine that women have the resources to encourage others.

Fertilize! Offer extra nutrition by taking the time to care about your mentee.

## Nourish with Practical Instruction

In today's fractured culture, some women simply crave an older woman's wisdom in everyday situations. Nancy says her relationship with Suzanne has helped her cope with life's everydayness as a mother of small children. Young women need to know they will survive the terrible twos, or how to handle the stress of earning a living. As an older woman shares from her life experience, a younger woman may grasp the hope that is offered. She

can see that this older woman has survived, and this gives
her hope.

However, the mentor doesn't have to be older to offer practical instruction. It is a woman's experience and ability to see the situation from another viewpoint that makes the difference. Her advice is like a second, and calmer, opinion.

The March 1996 issue of *Southern Living* contains a story called "Seeds of Survival."

> Beth [Adams] is an international development worker, a
> missionary. She specializes in helping village women in
> Malawi set up drip irrigation systems so they can grow
> food crops where none have thrived before. "You can't
> believe how hungry people are over there," she
> explains. "You'll hear someone out in your yard and
> ask them what they're doing, only to realize they're
> picking weeds to eat. Then you feel about this big."

Georgia-born Beth has come home to visit her postgraduate alma mater, in Fort Myers, Florida, ECHO, or Educational Concerns for Hunger Organization. ECHO has a small staff, who are assisted by college graduates serving as interns, to help run the farm. They take advantage of the steamy climate in that part of Florida to experiment in subtropical agriculture. The results are literally the seeds for survival in some countries. ECHO focuses on subsistence farming for countries around the globe, striving to use the tools at hand to improve local standards of living.

The article goes on to say that two-bucket kits in continuous production can raise enough food to feed a family of seven—all year long. She also teaches other agricultural tricks, such as burying banana stalks and manure together in trenches. In hot, humid climates, the two materials decompose in a couple of months and release phosphorous, potassium, and nitrogen into infertile soil. Crops planted on either side of the trench then take advantage of the windfall of rich nutrients.

Beth Adams becomes the fragrance of Christ in a dry and dusty land. In addition,

Beth, from the book
*The Language of
Flowers,* I give you a
bouquet of
Hawthorne, *hope,*
and Forget-Me-Nots,
*true love.*

the seeds that Beth planted through an irrigation system
became flowers of hope and food in someone else's garden.
Beth mentors through very practical instruction. She lives
among people who without her help may starve—you can't get
much more practical than teaching people how to survive in
harsh physical conditions. Beth, abiding in Christ, becomes a
branch of hope for starving people by sharing seeds of life in
Christ and seeds of life-giving food, nourishing the sprouts with
prayer, a caring presence, practical knowledge, and hope.

## Water and Fertilize

1. Mentors must abide in Christ, the source of nourishment.
2. Help mentees become connected to the true Vine,
   Christ. Or, if they are already connected, show them
   the way to abide and draw deeply on the nourishment
   Christ provides.
3. Water all you do with prayer, and teach mentees to
   draw from the well of prayer.
4. Fertilize the seedlings of the new life, energy, direction,
   and hope with vision and tender loving care.
5. Know and use the nourishing value of practical advice.

# IX

## *Protecting Plants*

Plants, especially young plants, need protection against frost, insects, disease, and weeds. Frost kills quickly, but most plants can be protected by a light covering of mulch. Insects are a pesky problem that may go unnoticed until it is too late. The good gardener will keep watch on her plants, checking under the leaves for eggs, and inspecting carefully for other signs of insects. Disease, such as a fungus, can often be stopped if caught early. Weeds, if they are allowed to grow, will choke the life out of plants.

Mentors can help protect their mentees just as the gardener can work to protect her plants.

### The Frost

The frost, or an attitude problem, will kill a relationship quickly. As a mentor, you can help protect the new growth in your mentee's life as well as in your relationship against attitude problems. One of the best ways is to establish an open line of communication early. The sooner you make it clear that you are open to talking about anything your mentee needs to talk about, the better off your relationship will be.

Often, attitude problems stem from a sense of not being heard or understood. If you establish a listening relationship early, you may be able to stave off future problems. Your mentee should feel free to talk to you, even if what she has to say is critical of you. You may not always agree in the end; but talk through the problem rationally, without flaring emotions, and end the discussion amicably. Help your mentee to see that her criticism does not affect your love and concern for her. She must know that you have truly listened to her, whether you agree or not.

If you sense an attitude problem, address it early. Initiate conversation and seek resolution to whatever may be causing the communication problem.

## Insects

A lack of confidence will eat a mentee like an insect. It will lay eggs of self-doubt that will hatch when you least expect it. Larvae may nibble away at her roots and cut her off from nourishment and water.

Be an encourager and lavish your mentee with praise. Show loyalty to her privately and in public. This is not to say that you should be false and flattering. Flattery is easy to spot and does nothing to bolster confidence. True praise and encouragement, on the other hand, will bring a smile to her face and deep sense of joy at being noticed and loved.

It always helped our family when one of my children's teachers or coaches bragged on them in front of the child. Believe me, it helped the child *and* the parent. You see, coaches and teachers can often see what parents can't see, because at times, we are too close to the situation. I thank God for teachers, coaches, aunts, and uncles who affirm the children on a regular basis. This, in the truest sense, is mentoring.

Growing up in a pastor's home, it was expected that each of the children take piano lessons. Only because of the generosity of my father's sister, Aunt Mary Milligan, did we get those piano lessons. Aunt Mary's life has continued to impact mine as through the years she has been a source of encouragement in my ministry with love, letters, and words fittingly spoken. If aunts and uncles take the opportunity, they can help families today by adding a different voice, enhancing the growth of nieces and nephews, and mentoring right alongside parents.

Constantly look for what is good and admirable in your mentee and bring it to her attention. Build her confidence. In so doing you will protect her against the feelings of self-doubt that will come when she fails—for she will surely fail at some things, as we all do. Show her how to responsibly use the gifts she has been given, and encourage her.

## Disease and Weeds

Disease will come to your garden at one time or another, but it can be prevented from spreading if you catch it early. To keep disease from spreading, the gardener will cut away the diseased portion of the plant, and, if this is not effective, she may have to resort to the use of chemicals.

Weeds, if allowed to grow, will choke the life out of a plant by preventing it from getting enough sunlight, drawing nutrients from the soil, and spreading its roots to prevent the desirable plant's roots from developing. Weeds must be dealt with early before they have a chance to grow.

Disease and weeds are the equivalent of sin in our lives. At some point, both you and your mentee will struggle with sin. It must be dealt with early.

Make sure you always deal with sin in your own life quickly. Nothing will spoil a mentoring relationship more quickly than sin in the mentor's life. Don't allow it. Continue to draw on your source of strength in the Vine, Christ.

And at all times, avoid judgment! "Do not judge. . . . How can you say to your [sister], 'Let me take the speck out of your eye,' when all the time there is a plank in your own eye? You hypocrite, first take the plank out of your own eye, and then you will see clearly to remove the speck from your [sister's] eye" (Matt. 7:1–5 NIV).

Once you have dealt with the sin in your own life, sin in your mentee's life will be easy to spot. But, do not judge her. Pray for her. Ask God to reveal to her the sin that needs to be pulled from her life. Study Scripture that will shine light on the sin and ask God to guide you in your dealings with your mentee. The Holy Spirit will pull the sin that blocks the Sonlight and cut out the disease before it has a chance to spread.

- Weeding a garden makes room for the flowers to grow.
- Weeding a life makes room for God's Spirit to flourish.

## Protecting Your Mentee

- Keep communication open to protect against feelings of not being heard and understood.
- Encourage and build confidence to protect against self-doubt.
- Deal with sin in your own life, pray, study the Scripture, and seek God's direction to protect your mentee against sin in her life.

# X

## Perfectly Pruned

The task of pruning produces optimal growth in a garden. This is also true in the lives of mentors and mentees. As God weeds and prunes our lives, He teaches us the sweetness of obedience. He then allows us to share with others in the mentoring process, in tending a garden life to bring glory to the Father.

One of my uncles was a fruit farmer, and he was always cutting away what looked like perfectly good bunches of grapes! He would trim branches and discard them. These barren trees looked so dead after he finished, and I thought they would never bear fruit again. I couldn't imagine how the grapes, full and lush, that were cut away could possibly change the grapes that were left.

In our yard, we prune the crepe myrtle trees, and they stand naked and without dignity all winter. One could get discouraged without knowing these trees will produce new growth and luscious flowers in the spring—filling in the garden, bringing beauty and shade.

Some years ago, a gardener told me to snip off some of the early buds on my chrysanthemums so that those that were left would be larger. With great fear, I did just that. She was right! The results were beautiful.

### Pruning Produces Better Fruit

The purpose of pruning is to enable the vine and the branches attached to that vine to grow the best possible fruit. The principles of viticulture relate to life. There are times when the vinedresser, the manager of the vineyard, has to prune beautiful and luscious grapes from certain vines so that branch will bear better fruit. When a branch bears too much fruit, the grapes on that branch will lack flavor and sweetness. The farmer takes off some of the beautiful grapes so that the ones remaining will be full of flavor and sweetness.

At times, God, my Vinedresser, indicates there are things in my life that have to go. This is certainly not out of meanness. It is necessary so the fruit that remains in my life will be sweet and full of flavor to honor and glorify Him.

As *The Message* says in John 15:5, "When you're joined with me and I with you, the relation [is] intimate and organic, the harvest is sure to be abundant."

When we abide in Christ, the Vine, it is out of this abiding that we have something to give. Only what we have received from the Vinedresser will be what others really want. Can you recall being drawn into the presence of a woman, only to discover it is *Christ* dwelling in her that draws you to her presence? Women will be drawn to a woman whose abiding relationship in Christ flowers and blossoms. It is Christ in her that others desire to know.

The Vinedresser now knows that the vine is prepared, and prunes it most drastically. What appears to be an unmerciful cutting away of all the beauty of the vine becomes the determining factor in the strength of the vine and the quality of the fruit that is to come.

When I dig deep into God's Word and the presence of God, my heart is preparing me for the storms of life. When the storm comes, I am drawn deep into the roots of my relationship in Him and find Him adequate.

The spring of 1996 presented a variety of storms in my own life. One day I received news that our son, David, had been diagnosed with cancer. This news drove me to the Word of God for solace and comfort.

The next morning in my abiding time, the Psalmist invited me to cast my burden upon the Lord. The verse says, "Cast what He has given you upon the Lord. He will never allow you to totter" (Psalm 55:22 *The Message*).

*WOW!* I wrote that in my prayer journal. That led me to Jeremiah 31:3–5 (NASB): "I have loved you with an everlasting love; Therefore I have drawn you with lovingkindness. Again I will build you, and you shall . . . plant vineyards."

I responded, "Yes, Lord! You are not through with David and his wife, Colleen." Peace came. That led me to Psalm 107:37 (NASB): "And sow fields, and plant vineyards, And gather a fruitful harvest."

My journal relates my journey through the Scripture during the next months while abiding in Christ, thanking God for His

promise that He would continue to work through the lives of
David and Colleen. The hymn given to me by the father of my
dearest friend was "Day by Day," words by Caroline Sandleberg
and this became my prayer. I sang it daily, and often on my
knees, in His presence: "Day by day and with each passing
moment, Strength I find to meet my trials here; Trusting in my
Father's wise bestowment, I've no cause for worry or for fear"—
abiding means embracing the pruning and trusting in my
Father's wisdom.

Remember, the purpose of pruning is to enable the vine and
branches attached to the vine to grow the best possible fruit.
Each year, vigorous new growth is accomplished by pruning.

Gardening books suggest it is best to prune in early spring
while the trees lie dormant. Pruning in the garden is a time-con-
suming task, but essential. Pruning fruit trees increases fruit pro-
ductivity and size. Always prune the damaged, dead, or diseased
limbs first. Trees and bushes can be pruned into many different
shapes. In your flower garden, cutting away dead leaves and
blossoms as they die not only improves the look of the plants,
but encourages new growth on the plant.

When God chooses to prune in our lives, it may come at any
season of life. After the pruning, the vinedresser watches carefully—waiting for the right time to pick the fruit.

A grapevine exists for one purpose alone: to bear the best
grapes—the fruit of the vine. This is true for Christians! This is
also true for mentors. The gifts—or fruits in the body of Christ—
are not for you personally, but they are for the body of Christ to
bring honor to Christ. That keeps us from claiming ownership
and helps us celebrate stewardship of God's gifts. When we
acknowledge His gifts in the body, we desire to help each gift
become all that God intended in the body, for the body, to
please Christ.

Many years ago, I had finished a lecture series on personal
relationships, and was visiting with my host in the car as he
drove me to the airport. He was very complimentary about my
presentation, but he asked if I would mind a critique. I was
somewhat new on the speaking circuit and I told him that I
would welcome his remarks.

He said, "You really do communicate well with college students. You are honest, humorous, and quite knowledgeable in
your subject matter—very important! But, you are probably not

aware of a habit that detracts from your message. Your message is very good and I don't want anything detracting from it as you speak. When you are getting a point across on a personal matter, like 'it's a man thing' or 'it's a woman thing,' you giggle and cover your mouth with your hand . . . almost like a little girl. It's cute, but only the first time."

I responded that I was aware that I was doing it, but certainly not aware it was detracting. I thanked him for risking to help me become a better speaker.

As the plane took off, I replayed the tape of my lecture in my head, and sure enough, *he was right!* I visualized my hands covering my mouth again and again. I smiled to myself, thinking I will be a better speaker because that campus minister cared enough to mentor me, carefully pruning a habit from my speaking style. Believe me, the next time I spoke, I worked very hard to break that habit. His courage with me has given me pruning permission with others, knowing they will grow to do their best.

Thank you,
Joe Baskins!

## Too Much Fruit? Too Busy?

When pruning, use courage, gentleness, and truth. Remember, it will impact the fruit of eternity, and the purpose in pruning is not to make the person look bad, but rather, to make the fruit of the vine look good.

Have you experienced times in your life when you became so busy you thought you could not go on for another moment? Even in ministry, whether lay ministry or professional, we live very cluttered and busy lives, always working to bear fruit, and then perhaps discovering that all the sweetness has gone from our life. It is possible to live in our family unit or to be in our work setting, consumed by business, and not be there for the very people we love and need the most.

When we bear too much fruit, the fruit of our lives is bland. Our lives become dull and we have no joy.

You may be a very talented person—the one everyone comes to in order to get things done—but they may not like being with you! The way we do things may cancel out the good if our bad attitude shows in the process. Haven't you heard yourself say, "I'm at a terrible place right now, and so far behind, I just can't get ahead. Just ignore my actions today!"

Women who produce too much fruit often complain about how heavy the branches are. Does your soul garden beg for pruning shears to cut things away?

In life, as with gardens, we experience seasons. Each season in the garden will take some pruning care. Leaves need to be raked in fall. Debris will need to be cleared away after a winter storm. Soil preparation comes in the early spring, and weeding certainly needs to be done in the summer. We also need pruning in every season of our lives.

Every season brings new challenges; but remember, each season brings life experience that is preparing you for the next turn in the road. Even in this busy season of life, you can be used of God to mentor another woman. Allow God to prune what is unnecessary from your life, so that the fruit you bear will be sweet. Perhaps your branches will yield sweet fruit in the life of another.

Older women, embrace each new season. I call you to draw deep from your roots in Christ and ask Him how you can use what He has taught you to mentor and walk beside another woman, gently exchanging life!

Everywhere that I have shared a bit about writing this book, I've been told, "We desperately need mentors, but find that older women are not willing to be mentors." I pray God will prune away that attitude if it is in your life . . . the Kingdom garden needs older women!

Have you ever been so tired you began to resent everything? Surely a pity-party followed—bland and joyless. You perhaps dreamed and prayed for a maid, knowing that with a maid, you could finally get ahead. If God had answered your prayer for a maid, would you continue in your unhealthy lifestyle, saying yes to everything and to everyone? What could be pruned from your life in order for you to experience the quiet centering of His presence, equipping you to handle what He chooses to leave in your life?

• What do you need to put down?
• What do you need to pick up?

Maybe you need pruning shears, not a maid service. I heard a well-known speaker recently make this statement: "I did not know how heavy my luggage was until I quit carrying it."

Vinedressing is not only helpful, it is absolutely essential for spiritual health and survival!

## Pruning in the Garden of Another

Like the garden, each new season in life needs pruning. I do not mean the seasons noted by the months of the year, but the seasons of our walk with God. John 15 states the theology of the vinedresser. God, the Vinedresser, is the Pruner. This is His task. If we take those sharp shears in our own hands, trying to prune in someone's life, we will likely cut too much or even prune in the wrong places . . . perhaps, even rendering permanent damage! We tend to be the hardest on ourselves. Let us lead women to let God prune in their lives through the truth of God's Word—taking the shears of God's love and clipping away unnecessary stuff from our lives.

In *The Secret Garden,* as Mistress Mary works in the garden—digging, planting, pruning, cutting back, adding, and watching the changes—she is at the same time doing all those things in the life of Master Colin. One evening, as Dickon and his mother sit together by his garden, she compliments him on his garden, and he says, "All a chap's got to do to make 'em thrive, mother. Be friends with 'em for sure. They're just like th' 'creatures.' If they're thirsty give 'em a drink and if they're hungry give 'em a bit o' food." Dickon goes on to tell his mother the whole story about the secret garden, Master Colin's recovery to health, and their plan to tell his father, Mr. Craven, when he returns to the manor. "My word!" she said. "It was a good thing that little lass came to th' Manor. It's been th' makin' o' her an' th' savin' o' him." You might be used of God in the same way in your mentee's life—if you will allow Him to use you, if you will abide in Christ!

When God, the true Vinekeeper, prunes, it hurts. In the natural vine, it is literally called *bleeding/tearing.* When the keeper of the vine cuts away from the branch the clusters of grapes to produce more growth, that branch bleeds—it loses sap. This is called *tearing.* The sap floods over the cut branch and it protects the branch from disease while it is healing.

How like God, our Father, to provide protection for the plant after pruning! He does the same for us. Psalm 147:3 (NASB) teaches, "He heals the brokenhearted, And binds up their wounds." Healing takes time in plants *and* in people. While healing, dig deep into God's Word for truth to assist the process, knowing that the Vinedresser makes all the difference. His purpose is: healthy vines deeply rooted in Christ, out of which His Spirit flows, expressing new life, new relationships, new fruit, and a greater desire to abide in Him.

Is your mentee so busy that she has lost her joy? Is she pulled in many directions at once? Everything she is doing may be good; but if she is so busy that she is unhappy, she may need your help.

Pray about each step in your mentoring relationship. Don't approach your mentee without first praying that God will guide you in all that you say and do.

- Talk to her about the importance of pruning. Tell her that by cutting away some of the good fruit, the gardener makes it possible for the remaining fruit to be larger and sweeter.
- Help her to draw some conclusions about the fruit in her own life. By taking on so many good projects, is she limiting the sweetness and size of the results?
- Ask her to project what the best possible fruit could be from all her efforts, and then select the fruits that will give her the most long-term pleasure.
- Suggest that the other projects might be eliminated or cut away, so that the remaining projects will bear incredible fruit.
- Once she has made her decisions, set up some form of accountability and help her find ways to achieve her goals.

## Where Is Your Trust?

While Jesus was speaking, everywhere the people looked, they saw vines. Vines were pictured on the coins of that day. A vine was synonymous with the Nation of Israel. In John 15:2 (NASB), Jesus talks about vine growth. He says, "Every branch in Me that does not bear fruit, He takes away; and every branch that bears fruit, He prunes it, that it may bear more fruit."

It is easy in our culture to trust _things_. It is easy in life to trust ourselves. Most of us find it is easier to do something—anything, rather than to trust God. Ask yourself this very hard question: What are the things in my life that I trust more than I trust Christ?

It might be trusting in material possessions. We must learn to hold our possessions loosely and teach our mentees to do the same. What might happen if this generation of women chooses to hold their possessions loosely and to intentionally live to bear fruit, following the One Who said, "Leave everything and trust Me?"

If our purpose is to help all persons grow toward a God-centered lifestyle, one that offers every person the opportunity to hear and respond to the gospel, then we will need to consider leaving some things behind. We might consider living simply in order to help someone simply live.

Is simple living something that rings true to you? Could you help another woman to see the truth in the concept of living simply in order to live more fully for God? What could be pruned from your life that would enable you to dedicate more of your time and resources to helping others and serving God?

Help your mentee to think through these questions if she is a Christian. If she is not a Christian, the concept might be hard for her to understand from a spiritual perspective. However, there are many good books about simple living written from a secular perspective; the benefits of simple living aren't solely spiritual. Explain all of the benefits of simple living to your mentee, including the reasons why you, as a Christian, practice simple living.

## Saying *No!*

We should not expect the pruning process to be painless. Saying *No!* is difficult. God's pruning is to improve the beauty, the flavor, and the sweetness of the fruit that we bear in each new season of life. When the gardener prunes, the vine reaches deep into its roots, drawing on everything within the root system to produce more fruit. The vine responds naturally to the pruning process by producing even better fruit—and more of it.

That is why the Word of God is so vital in our lives. When we are wounded by life or the pruning of an event, circumstance, or habit from our lives, we must dig deep into God's Word for comfort, direction, and healing. We must rest assured that the Father has a purpose for cleansing the things, habits, or attitudes from our lives—so that the fruit that remains will be sweet and real to us and to others.

In *Making Choices,* Alexandra Stoddard includes a chapter titled, "The Art of No." Stoddard says, "Once you have decided what you wish to do, what you believe is the *right* thing under the circumstances, no allows you to weed out what is redundant, excessive, inappropriate, or conflicting."

*No* is a hard word to say. I struggle with the word. I practice it often in front of the mirror, until I get the *maybe* out of my voice.

Driven, faced with endless choices and multiple activities, enslaved by color-coded calendars—we are people who struggle to do it all. Stoddard makes this great statement: "The art of 'no' is a bit easier when you remember that you can be only one place at a time."

In family, ministry, and community, everyone deals with the pressure and the manipulation of two words: *ought* and *should*. The ability to say *no* is releasing, empowering! Women must learn to examine external pressure, to be empowered to choose. Pruning us helps lay aside even a much-loved activity with people about whom we really care, in order to choose the best fruit God has for us. See yourself as part of the body of Christ, trusting that the *whole* body does the work and is not reliant only on you to accomplish its ministry.

Saying *yes* is often related to our own expectations as well as the expectations and opinions of others. We believe we can do it all, while perhaps we need the affirmation and appear to have it all together. The truth is simple: *no* is realistic. It helps us determine what is important and what is the best possible use of our giftedness. John 8:31–32 (NASB) says this: "Jesus therefore was saying to those Jews who had believed Him, 'If you abide in My word, then you are truly disciples of Mine; and you shall know the truth, and the truth shall make you free.'"

*Truth* is the person of Jesus . . . the One Who extends the invitation to abide. Imagine looking into the face of Jesus when you say *no* or *yes*. Abiding in the person of truth makes you free to say . . .

- No!—to activity
- No!—to external pressure
- No!—to expectations

- Yes!—to abiding
- Yes!—to fruit bearing
- Yes!—to clinging to the vine

Pruning in the garden takes many shapes and forms, while enhancing its growth and beauty. When a plant dies, the gardener takes it out of the garden.

I won't soon forget June 1996. Walking early that morning in my front garden, I pulled out some lifeless plants that had not made it through the overnight rains. They were waterlogged—they had literally drowned! I wanted to wring the water from what was left of their root system. I felt so helpless.

Later that same morning, I learned my mother had but a few days to live. The life was literally draining out of her tired body after having struggled with Alzheimer's for a few years. She was no longer able to accept nutrients necessary to keep her alive. As I sat in front of my mirror and made up my face that morning, I listened to a concert tape of the Florida Baptist Singing Men and Singing Women as they sang "Majesty, Worship His Majesty!" I began to cry. How gracious of God to use music to minister to me that lonely morning. As their music filled the room, I heard His whisper: "I have her home ready. She will now be in my presence. Release her, Esther, to my garden." Peace came. So, just as my garden heart has one less plant, so heaven's garden looks all the better because my mother has entered the presence of His Majesty! I am sure that any daughter is never ready to release her mother, but I knew Mother was ready to be released from the disease that finally took her life.

Recently I have experienced a season of pruning in my life. August 28, 1995, Bob and I celebrated our 37th wedding anniversary. I persuaded Bob to attend a marriage encounter weekend with me as part of the celebration. The weekend was an intense 44 hours all about couple love. We learned to talk and write about our feelings. I relearned many things about marriage in general and about my marriage in particular. I learned that I was to be the very presence of Christ to my husband.

First Peter 3:1–2 (NASB) says, "In the same way, you wives, be submissive to your own husbands so that even if any of them are disobedient to the word, they may be won without a word by the behavior of their wives, as they observe your chaste and respectful behavior."

What a huge assignment! In the everyday stuff of life, I am to live with my Bob in such a way that I am the very presence of Christ to him. I wept. Far too seldom had that been true in our relationship. Memories flashed across my mind like a color video—showing my actions the last time I came home from a speaking trip . . . exhausted . . . and took my weariness out on the very one I love the most.

One of the couples shared what it means to be *married single*. That might be a husband putting golf or sports before his marriage, . . . or a wife putting children, garden club, or a career before her husband. A person in professional ministry might spend more time on the church than on the marriage. *Married single* is when a married couple lives as if single, doing their own thing—perhaps not even realizing the drastic consequences. It is when other people, interests, or concerns take priority over the relationship.

My husband had said to me—on more than one occasion—'Honey, you know when you come home exhausted, I love taking care of you and putting you back together—but then I give you away again, and they always get your best and I get what's left."

Oops! There's an issue for pruning shears. I never heard the last four words in his sentence: 'I get what's left." You see, I was only listening to the part about how much he loved me.

I tasted the heavy weariness of packed suitcases, crowded airplanes and airports, hotels, of clothes washed or dry cleaned and then repacked. I began a quiet *letting go* of my self-inflicted travel schedule. I saw the glaring truth. My husband was not first in my life, next to Christ. My work was! Calendars don't lie! All justifications melted. All rationalizations dissolved under the loving eyes of His scrutiny. The pruning was radical. Changes had to come. Peace finally came.

It's been a year. Peace remains. God used my husband and others to prune the unnecessary elements from my life, elements that hindered my effectiveness in ministry; my joy as a Christian, a wife, and a mother; and my ability to offer my husband the love and time he deserved.

One of the most empowering things you can teach your mentee is how to say *no*. Show her how to distinguish between activity that is good and activity that *she needs* to be involved in. Show her how to avoid the guilt and need for approval that causes people to say *yes* to requests, even when they really don't have time to do the job well.

## Pruning Is Painful, But the Results Are Sweet!

When our Father, the Vinedresser, prunes us, it is always to place the fruits of His Spirit in our lives.

He places *desire* for Himself *into* our activity.
He places *serenity* into our schedules.
He places *quietness* over our noise.
He places *joy* beside our sorrow.
He places *love* around our hate.
He places *humility* within our pride.
He places *obedience* in our disobedience.
He places *peace* through our rebellion.
He places *Himself* into our hearts.

When we release and let go of that which deadens our lives, God makes us joyful and effective once again.

### Principles of Pruning

1. Pruning in a human life means cutting away that which hinders the growth of what is best in that life.
2. God must be the One to decide what needs to be pruned in your mentee's life; but God can use you to help her see the areas that need to be pruned.
3. Teach your mentee to trust in God, not in material wealth, for satisfaction. A simplified lifestyle will eliminate much of what drives us into the rat race.
4. One of the most empowering things you can teach your mentee is how to say *no.*
5. Pruning may be painful, but the glorious sweetness of the fruit produced by this process makes it all worthwhile.

# XI

## *Supplying Support*

Everyone needs to hear encouragement and feel valued. Pray with your mentee often. Share with her what you think is her greatest strength. What a treasured gift this can be. It is like getting a bouquet of spring flowers. Any room in your home takes on a new look in the presence of the bouquet. What power we have to enhance the look of a person's life!

### Value Her with Encouragement

My friend, Patches Row, tells the following story: "A gentle and humble woman who had taught me in Sunday School since my days in the nursery, walked up behind me on the porch of my home church one Sunday night. She placed her hands on my shoulders and quietly said, 'It is true I don't remember a lot about you; but I have seen glimpses of who you can be and I like what I've seen.' That made me feel ten feet tall, which is quite a feat for someone who would have to be put on a rack for long sessions to truly claim five feet, two inches!"

Patches continues, "Harriette Weeks was a mentor to me, and she taught me the same thing Calvin Miller says in *The Empowered Leader:* 'The world is not generally helped along by people who are driven to understand themselves but by people who want to change the world.'"

### Value Her with Prayer Support

Perhaps the greatest mentoring that my parents did with my five brothers and sisters was their habit of praying daily for each child by name and with a specific petition. My mother's prayers were direct and to the point.

Not long ago we had a weekend visit from our dear friends, Paul and Nicole Johnson. I could not wait for Nicole to see my garden.

Prior to their arrival, I was delighted to find plant name markers in a gardening book. I ordered them and as soon as they arrived, I carefully printed the names of each flower group in my garden on the markers, placing the marker by each flower for easy identification.

When Paul and Nicole arrived, I immediately showed her my garden. She looked around and said all the right things! As she bent over to look at the markers, I heard her say, "Dusty Miller, Heather, Salvia . . . Oh, wow—are these the people you pray for?"

How I wished I could have said *yes*. I explained that those were the names of all my plants.

She laughed and replied, "Well, knowing you, I thought they were people, perhaps missionaries, for whom you pray."

What a wonderful idea for you gardeners. Add the names of your children, grandchildren, adopted neighborhood children, sponsored Third-World children, friends, co-workers, or missionaries to your flower garden by name! As you sit and rest near your garden, cover them in prayer. Remember, when you pray, God's power is released.

In a recent issue of *Journey*, a devotional magazine for women, Selma Wilson wrote this as her editorial:

> I have two daughters. Each night, we take turns having our family prayertime in our daughters' rooms kneeling at their beds. It is part of our family tradition. Sometimes during the night, after the girls are asleep, Rodney will go into their rooms and kneel beside their beds and pray over them. He's been doing this since they were babies. One of my most precious childhood memories is of the special prayertime Mother would have with me and my brothers before we went to school. Prayer and mothers. They seem to go together. But I often ask myself, "Who is praying for our country, our homes, our children? Or are we depending on someone else to do the praying? If so, who?"[1]

Imagine the fragrance of Christ, pouring from a women's group as they adopt a young family in the church and perhaps one from a community day-care center, covenanting to pray for that young family for one year.

As you support your mentee through prayer, remember to pray for her friends and family, and anyone else she comes in contact with on a regular basis. Surround all she does with prayer. Have a special place where you go to pray for her each day. And pray for her throughout the day, each time she comes to your mind. What better way could there be to ensure the growth and success of your mentee than by asking God to work in her life and the lives of those she knows?

## Value Her with Written Support

My husband, Bob, has a most wonderful mentoring gift. He is a master letter writer.

If Bob attends a conference as a guest or as a participant, nearly everyone on the program will receive a note of encouragement from him as soon as the event is over. His notes are short, to the point, and full of love, affirmation, and encouragement. I know! I've received many from him. This letter-writing ministry imparts joy to the writer and the receiver. By writing letters, you savor the memory about which you are writing and help others create treasured memories.

I have friends who keep *love note* folders. They tell me they dip into the file on the tough days just to feel the written hug of love or bouquet of compliments. I confess—I do the same thing!

I see note writing as a ministry in the marketplace and family, and definitely as a part of mentoring. It is seeing someone do something special and then responding with:

- a written note of thanks through the mail;
- a self-adhesive note left on the computer;
- a card on a car window;
- a note in the lunch bag;
- a joy letter expressing affirmation;
- a card acknowledging another's struggle;
- a love message on voice mail.

Written notes, like daisies in a vase, can last in the heart for weeks. The written word can be read over and over, giving the heart time to cherish the words. Reading a letter of encouragement and love feels like sitting in a garden of beauty and breathing in the fresh air, breathing out anxiety, and taking time to rest in the stillness of kindness expressed.

A note written to a child or sweetheart on a dry erase board placed on the refrigerator can bring a smile as well as lift a burden. We have a heart-shaped dry erase board on our refrigerator.

All spring, Bob and I had continually written love notes to each other. After a recent visit from our grandchildren, I noticed the latest message had been wiped off and replaced by a love note from our granddaughter. That message stayed almost all summer, bringing delight each time we passed the refrigerator door.

## Value Her with Support in the Hard Times

I have been involved for five years in a mentoring relationship with an exceptional young mother. It began as we walked together in the early morning hours. Our hearts, desiring the things of God, drew us together. I was there for the birth of her children, the struggle in marriage, spiritual growth, and just good friendship. Neither of us knew where the garden path of friendship would take us.

I listened to the unraveling of a marriage, and the hurt and fear that robs life of eternal promises made and not kept. Our heart for the things of God has kept us in touch, even though we now live in different cities.

I recently learned from this friend about a program called Crossroads. My reaction was to ask this haunting question, "Why hasn't the church led in this type of ministry?"

Crossroads is an ongoing, grant-funded program offered by a community college in Florida for women beginning again. The Crossroads staff consists of warm and caring professional women, whose primary aim is to help women explore their options and build their self-esteem through directed group discussion, classroom exercises, and individual counseling. Crossroads can help:

- the newly separated, divorced, or widowed homemaker make the transition into the paid workforce, schooling, or community;
- the woman whose husband's disability is putting a strain on their income and relationship;
- the single parent struggling to meet the many demands made by inadequate income;
- the homemaker displaced by the empty-nest syndrome.

Crossroads is a career redevelopment program for women who are beginning again. Every day for two weeks women are immersed in esteem building, career evaluation, career counseling, and employment skills. Though this program is federally funded, it relies heavily on volunteer help. This help ranges from graduates of the program to professional women in the marketplace who, at one time or another, have experienced a *crossroad* in their life—a crossroad which has uniquely empowered them to help someone else in a crossroad journey.

These professional women join the classes to share their stories. My friend told me that these same professional women make a covenant with women entering the program that their call for help will be answered in 24 hours or less. That impressed me profoundly. No wonder the program works and has successful graduates. This is truly mentoring in the marketplace and making a difference.

Not long after my friend told me about Crossroads, I found the answer to my question of why the church hasn't led out in this type of ministry. It has! Christian Women's Job Corps (CWJC), a ministry of Woman's Missionary Union (WMU), is a great example of women mentoring other women in some of the same ways as the Crossroads program—and it's happening all across our nation. Several pilot projects are being conducted!

Camille Simmons has played a large role in the Christian Women's Job Corps pilot project in San Antonio, Texas. As Camille described what was happening through the love of Christians in San Antonio, I thought, *Yes! There it is! The Church is alive and well in San Antonio . . . mentoring these women . . . supporting them and helping them help themselves! Yes!*

According to Camille, the San Antonio Baptist Association Woman's Missionary Union and Buckner Benevolence joined forces to start this CWJC pilot project. It is a ten-week program in which they use a curriculum developed by Texas A&M to help women get into the job market.

"Linda Gwathmey is the program coordinator and head teacher," she said. "WMU helps by bringing in volunteers from across the association, who do everything from teaching, providing lunch, and donating needed items.

"The second ten-week class was truly extraordinary," Camille continued. "Most of the women were in their forties . . . trapped in the system for the first time in their lives. The death of a spouse, illness, divorce, and/or job loss brought about the circumstances. Six of the women were living in the Salvation Army shelter."

One of the women from this group, who calls herself Star,

showed up early to learn computers. She was anxious to start learning this skill that she knew would help her in getting a job!

"Star lives at the Salvation Army women's shelter, and her husband lives at the men's shelter," Camille said. "Once a week, he sells plasma so they will have a little bit of money to buy necessary toiletries."

One day, Camille learned that Star needed $40 to take the last part of the GED test. Star did not ask Linda or the volunteers for the money.

"She went to her classmates," Camille said. "And working together, they called in every loan they could and came up with the $40. Tears came to my eyes as I realized what they had accomplished. They had bonded into a very caring support group. They had sacrificed to help one of their own—and don't forget—six of them live in the shelter."

In May of each year, the San Antonio Baptist Association holds a recognition banquet for its volunteers. Many important people come to pay tribute to those who are volunteering their services to the community.

For this particular year, Camille and Linda devised a plan that would enable the women from the CWJC class to attend the banquet. The women in the class enlisted volunteers from the churches to help them get dressed for the occasion. They helped each other with their nails and hair, and on the night of the banquet "in walked ten lovely women, along with Linda and some of the volunteers. I placed them at two tables—one with the mayor, and the other with a state representative. The women told me later that they felt like Cinderella at the ball."

A vase of Chinese Chrysanthemums, *cheerfulness under adversity*, to the women in Christian Women's Job Corps!

Star is now serving as an intern in the Association's office, getting work experience and moving into the job market. What a beautiful example of the church in action this is! Loving Christian women volunteered to help mentor and train women who were having a hard time surviving. And through their love and support, these women have now learned how to help themselves, as well as how to help and support each other. It is love that creates a chain reaction!

Earlene Jessee, director of a women's organization in Virginia, told me of several other great examples of how the Church is responding to the need for mentors in our world. Two examples of how they are reaching out in their communities are

• The Dorcas Project—Goal: to seek to address homelessness and poverty across the Commonwealth of Virginia. They believe they must become actively involved in bringing hope to this seemingly hopeless situation. This is being done in: one church; one family; transitional housing; rescue food and clothing programs; community gardens; community job banks; and educational programs.

• The Ruth and Naomi Project—Goal: this project provides the opportunity to create one-to-one relationships between experienced leaders and young leaders within the group's membership. Their purpose is to provide older, more experienced leaders an opportunity to pass on to the next generation their love for missions, leadership skills, and abilities. At the same time, young leaders have an opportunity to develop systematically the skills and leadership abilities to lead their organization as it enters the next century. This is a deliberate, formal, two-year mentoring program that will impact the Kingdom of God.

These women are networking with community organizations already at work to make a difference—what a beautiful example this is of Christian women modeling a true New Testament church for their local community. Consider the women's organization of your church, and ask yourself if it is touching the body of Christ, or the world, or both—or neither?

## Accountability

By asking frequently for updates, you build accountability into the mentoring relationship. You cannot properly mentor anyone without some accountability. Ask for updates on their spiritual progress, work-related efforts, academic accomplishments, family life, friendships, physical challenges, and any other areas that the two of you are working on. Holding your mentee accountable is very important to the mentoring relationship.

## Support Her by Listening

I asked Mary Lou Serratt, a strong Christian leader who has been

a mentor to her daughter, what advice she
could give to other mothers about mentoring
their children. She responded with these words:

"First, become the person God wants you to
be. This is an ongoing process of growth.
Then, help your child discover who she/he is
in God and His plans for her/him. Then listen.
Listen. Listen. Talk . . . sometimes! Expect the
best. Enjoy the present and anticipate a good
future."

This is good advice for all mentors. When
you are asking for life updates, listen, listen,
listen . . . and *always* expect the best.

Oodles and boodles
of Rose, Gloire de
Dijou, *a message of
love.* Thank you, Mary
Lou Serratt, for your
message of love to
your family and to us.

## Be Available for Friendship

By being available you assure your mentee that you will help
her reach her goals.

I was a young mother with a four-year-old daughter and a
brand new baby boy. We were living in a temporary apartment,
waiting for the loan to clear to be able to buy our first home. I
was told that the Mack Brown family lived just two blocks away,
and that Faye Brown would be dropping by to visit me.

Weeks went by and I did not see Faye. Then I heard that she
had experienced a bout with cancer and was home recovering.
It was time for cultivation in this garden bed of friendship. I
reached out to her with a chocolate cake. I thought I was just
taking a cake to a new friend. I had no idea what this woman
and her family would come to mean to me and to my family!

Faye was and is, in the truest sense of the word, a mentor-
friend to me. I cannot remember a time that Faye was too busy
to accept my phone call or my cry for help. It was Faye who
just happened by our new home early one morning offering to
help me *tidy up.*

I suggested we just have coffee. "Yes," she said, but first, she
began to make the beds and pick up toys. She was my elder
and I did not want her to work alone, so I joined in. We had
such a good time together.

We finished just as all my new church friends came through
the front door, arriving with housewarming gifts and sharing a
great deal of Texas hospitality!

What a gift Faye was to my life during our years of ministry in Texas. I sat in her *College of Kitchen Table Knowledge* many mornings, gleaning from her wisdom and insight.

In all these years of friendship with the Brown family, I never heard Faye Brown say an unkind word about anyone—ever! What a mentor she was to me . . . and still is! She certainly offered me the gift of friendship, and it all began because a younger woman baked a cake for a woman a few years older. It was her availability to me that made all this possible. What if Faye had been too busy to sit and talk to me over coffee, or too busy to *pop in* and help me *tidy up* before my new church family dropped by?

White Verbena, meaning *pure and guileless,* for Faye.

## Be Available to Support

The day I was writing this material, my phone rang. It was one of the young mothers in my church.

"What are you doing?" she asked.

I said that I was writing. She was aware from previous conversations that I was writing this mentoring book. She said that she was following up on my open invitation to find time to teach a group of the young women in our church. We settled on a date, and then I asked about a secret special weekend she had planned to be away with her husband. Everything had gone well. She excitedly told me about it and thanked me for the suggestion I had given in a recent marriage seminar. There was a long pause.

I understood from the pause that she had other questions. Sure enough, 30 minutes later, I had listened to her heart as she shared her struggle with a particular issue. I promised to pray for her and hoped I was encouraging to her.

When I hung up the phone, I said to myself, *Cheryl has chosen me as a mentor.* I thought about how she had pursued my friendship. I am certainly richer because this young mother reached out to me. It felt like having my own daughter in the same town.

It was my availability that made her feel comfortable with me. If, at some point, I had told her that I was too busy to talk or had not shown interest in her, she probably would not have sought my advice or friendship. You must make yourself available to your mentee.

## Be Available for Evaluation

In any event or relationship, we must evaluate with and for our mentees. Through evaluation you can decide what is working and what is not. Help your mentee through this process. One of your tasks in mentoring is to increase the effectiveness of the mentee's giftedness.

### Providing Support

- Pray for your mentee daily. Have a regular time and place to pray for her. Pray for her briefly as she comes to mind.
- Pray for your mentee's friends and family.
- Encourage your mentee regularly. Written notes are especially important because they can be saved and referred to later.
- Support your mentee during the hard times. For example, if she is having a hard time getting to school because she can't afford a baby-sitter, help her by baby-sitting, or find someone who can.
- Ask for frequent updates on your mentee's progress, and offer encouragement to keep her from losing heart.
- Listen and always expect the best.
- Make yourself available to your mentee at all times.
- Make time to evaluate the mentoring relationship.

# Part Four
# Releasing the Fragrance

# XII

## *Fragrant Bouquets*

On almost *any* occasion, women like to receive flowers as well as give them. Flowers bring cheer and comfort into almost any setting. Their fragrance enhances a room, begging for attention. Hardly anyone can pass a fresh bouquet without a comment.

Gardeners will tell you that much of the joy of gardening is sharing the content of the garden. It is a wonderful gift. You invest in the work of gardening, which is fulfilling to you, and you divide the product as you share the fragrance of the bouquet or fruit, which is fulfilling to others.

> A flower enhances a room for days.
> A garden enhances a home for months.
> A mentor enhances a life for eternity.

We are challenged by Paul's words in 2 Corinthians 2:14–15*a* (*The Message*): "Everywhere we go, people breathe in the exquisite fragrance. Because of Christ, we give off a sweet scent, rising to God, which is recognized by those on the way of salvation."

Imagine being the very fragrance of Christ—like a bouquet presented to your world.

Do you remember the distinct aroma of your grandmother or the fragrance of a woman in your church? When they pass by, the fragrance lingers. When you pass someone, are they touched by the fragrance of Christ in you? Imagine—through you, they have breathed in the exquisite fragrance of Christ. Ahh!

Warren Weirsbe, in his book *On Being a Servant of God,* gives this definition of ministry that I would like to plant in your heart: "Ministry takes place when divine resources meet human needs through loving channels to the glory of God."

I laughed to myself when I read this powerful statement: "Too many of us in ministry think God called us to be manufacturers, when He really called us to be distributors."

One of the greatest joys of being a follower of Christ is knowing that God takes the gifts He has given us, divides them, and His Kingdom is changed forever. In the passage about the boy who gives up his bread and fish for Christ to divide among the crowd, the Scripture says, "And they all ate and were satisfied" (Mark 6:42 NASB). We are called to distribute what God has put in our hands. Think of it like a bouquet from your life garden given to enhance another's life.

Through mentoring, we may give our gifts to the relationship, but the results will be so much more than what we put in. The results will be what we have given, divided, and multiplied by God, and released in the sweet fragrance of a garden life that blossoms and grows for the world to see and smell.

## It's So Sweet!

Remember the reference from Jeremiah where God says He plants His people, Israel? Imagine the mentoring difference women can make if we allow God to plant in us and teach our mentees to allow the same. The difference is that "their life shall be like a watered garden" (Jer. 31:12 NASB). A well-watered garden radiates beauty because of the work of the Gardener's hands. If we rely on God and teach our mentee to rely on God, He will satisfy her needs and she will become like "a watered garden, And like a spring of water whose waters do no fail" (Isa. 58:11b NASB).

In gardening, mulching done in the spring carries the garden into summer and winter. In summer, the mulch holds the moisture, which nurtures the plants. In winter, it protects the plant bed from severe weather.

In mentoring, we work in one season of a person's life and may not see the results until a much later season—if ever! Don't let that discourage you. That's the excitement in the spiritual journey. It is all to bring honor to God. We must remember that God can see what we cannot.

On the other hand, you may see mentoring results quickly. Allow me to add a word of caution at this point. When we mentor young women and recognize their leadership skills, we must be careful not to push them too quickly to the forefront. If they do not have time to mature, the results can be *quick success* and *quick failure*.

I recently learned of a church that seeks to develop leaders.

They require future leaders in their women's program to take one year of Bible study and discipleship training before they can serve in a leadership position. I call that earning the right to be heard! What a strong leadership base they are building. If a woman desires to become a leader in this church, she commits for one year. In leadership development, that is mentoring at its best.

When you are allowed to see mentoring results, the fragrance is sweet. It's like walking down a garden path on a warm summer evening and smelling the sweet scent of jasmine drifting by on the breeze!

I first met Earl Ann Lennert Bumpas when she was a college student and I was her campus minister. I quickly observed that she was a quiet, graceful woman. She was serving on a campus ministry committee. My observation was that her team did a consistently good job—very thorough, always following through with their assignments, and developing community in the process—under her capable leadership.

As we approached the fall, I invited her to take the leadership of the mid-winter retreat. I can remember her surprised response: "Do you really think I can do that?"

I assured her she could, and pointed out her strengths as a leader. She went to work, checking things with me, but only when necessary. I watched in delight at her excitement in the planning process and finally, directing the weekend. When it was over, she thanked me for believing in her and told me it helped her find her gifts.

As her mentor, I recognized the *seeds* of leadership in her life, her love for Christ and people, and her uniqueness in Christ. I shared the *nutrients* of encouragement and the *support* of prayer and a helping hand. I *watered* her gifts in giving her an opportunity and place for them to be exercised. She *blossomed* in leadership. She is now a pastor's wife in a Western state, and works with young women in her church.

Bob and I are often overwhelmed as we watch hundreds of students from our nearly ten years of service on the faculty at Samford University find their gifts as leaders. They are making a worldwide flower garden as they serve all over the world in professional and ministry careers.

Their combined impact really hit me during a commissioning service for new missionaries which I co-emceed. As the other emcee and I alternately announced the names of the missionary candidates, they took their places on the stage. I was told to keep my eye on the candidates as they passed in front of me and to keep the flow steady.

The very first couple took me by surprise. I recognized them from my Samford days. Of course, I wanted to run and hug their necks. But I couldn't do that because the event was being videotaped! Instead, I promised myself I would do it as soon as the evening ended.

My heart was not at all prepared to see a second Samford couple, nor the third or fourth, and most certainly not the eighth Samford student pass in front of my eyes. The TV camera caught the tears flowing freely down my face. I continued to read name after name—all the while, remembering that God had allowed us to work in His harvest field.

I challenge you to weep over the seeds that God calls you to plant . . . asking for a harvest and not caring who receives the credit. After all, it is His field, and He is calling for the harvest.

## Working Yourself Out of a Job

I will never forget the interview I once had for a position at a mission board. The interviewer and my future supervisor was Don Hammonds. He asked penetrating questions about my family, my background, and my gifts. He asked me what I did to play? Little did I know how much I would begin to learn about the balance of work and play. His next statement, however, surprised me.

"My job as your supervisor is to help you outgrow this job and move on to something else," he said.

That statement defines the art of mentoring. A strong standard for all mentors to follow is to help someone move to a new season of maturity and leadership and to celebrate the dividends for the Kingdom. Mentors help their mentees grow beyond them. Ted W. Engstrom says, "If a mentor is not stretching his protégé, he does not have a mentoring relationship."

Six years under Don's leadership shaped the future direction of my life. He could see in me what I could not see in myself.

We met consistently to look at our goals and performance standards. He knew when to push ahead and when to pull back. I'm an enthusiastic visionary and he consistently redirected my focus based on my stated goals. I looked forward to his input in my work.

After six years, he noticed a statement I'd written on my evaluation, saying that I was feeling stymied. He said, "I told you that you would outgrow this job. Let's pray about your gifts and something opening up here at the Board. Selfishly, I'd like to keep you on the staff."

Months later I was asked to consider a consulting position at the mission board, related to women in evangelism. As soon as I finished the interview, I immediately went to Don's office to discuss the interview with him.

Always the mentor, he asked me some hard questions. I kept these questions in a file with all the other bits and pieces of Don's wisdom. From that file, I'll share with you his handwritten questions to me . . . a treasure of our mentor/mentee years.

Don Hammond's bouquet to my life has been full of John Hopper Rose, *encouragement;* Single Rose, *simplicity;* and Gsmunda, *vision.* Thank you, Don!

## Questions for Evaluation
- What are you leaving behind? What is left undone?
- What have you accomplished?
- What are you going to? What are the new challenges?
- What did you want to do when you came to this present job?
- What do you want in a change?
- Will this happen in the new job better than it is happening in your present job?
- What are the strengths you carry to your new position?
- Do your talents, hopes, and dreams intersect with the new position?
- What are the advantages and disadvantages of leaving or staying?
- What changes will it make in terms of family?
- What do you think you will miss most as you leave this area of responsibility?
- What do you think will be your greatest gain in the new responsibility?

This kind of gardening in a person's life develops mentees into mentors. In the planning stages of your mentoring relationship, you and your mentee need to set a time to reevaluate and possibly end the relationship. This evaluation time provides a chance for either party to gracefully back out, or to redefine the relationship if it is to continue. These would be good questions to ask as you evaluate the progress of the relationship.

Think of the *Kingdom influence* this mentoring will have. I wish everyone could experience the positive mentoring I was given. Don planted in my life. He empowered me to grow. He taught me to multiply myself. He celebrated my accomplishments.

Matthew 26:6–13 is one of the times we see Mary of Bethany at the feet of Jesus, pouring perfume on His feet, and wiping it with her hair. Some in the room criticized, saying that the money should have been used for the poor. Jesus told them that the whole world would know of her act of worship toward Him. What a beautiful thought for those of us who serve and who mentor. What if you and I considered everything we do as an offering laid at the feet of Christ?

As your mentoring relationship draws to a close, rejoice in the beauty that God has allowed you to be a part of creating. Rejoice in the fragrance that spills out of a confident and fruitful life.

## Releasing the Fragrance

1. Through mentoring, we may give our gifts to the relationship, but the results will be so much more than what we put in.
2. We work in one season of a person's life and may not see the results until a much later season—if ever! Don't let that discourage you.
3. Be careful not to push your mentee too quickly to the forefront. If she does not have time to mature, the results can be quick success and quick failure.
4. You must work to stretch your mentee, working yourself out of a job.
5. Take the time to evaluate what has been accomplished and help your mentee to think about what her next step will be.
6. Celebrate your mentee's accomplishments and rejoice in the fragrance that is being released on the world.

# XIII

## *Garden Dividends*

During a visit with my father in Canada not long ago, he took me to his wonderful garden so that we could have a quiet visit together. As we talked, he bent down and pulled a carrot from the ground, scrubbed it clean with the carrot top greens, and handed it to me to eat. I'd seen him do this before. I felt like a little girl once again . . . except this time, I wasn't swiping the carrot, so afraid he'd catch me! He was actually giving it to me.

Always the teacher, he walked me to the fence of my sister's garden and showed me a plant. The plant was covered with pods, all absolutely packed with seeds.

He said, "If she doesn't cut these back, this plant will take over the garden next season, and destroy the balance. The truth is the pods could be picked and some of the seed replanted for a balanced garden."

What a photograph of the Word of God as seed in our lives. The plant was literally covered with pods. Each pod was full and ripe, ready to drop seeds into the soil. I felt that if I'd stayed a moment longer, I might have seen the process. Think of the eternal fruits of women like yourself who are

- rich in life experience;
- accepting God-given gifts;
- saturated in God's Word;
- empowered by God's Holy Spirit;
- bursting to spill over;
- giving life and eternally enhancing the Kingdom of God through *your* endowments.

And now imagine the garden you have planted in the life of your mentee—this same process will take place if you have been a faithful gardener. The seed dies . . . is buried in the soil . . .

and then, springs to life. It blossoms, as the process of mentoring continues to reproduce in others what has been planted in us.

The time will come when what you have planted and watched grow in the life of your mentee will begin to go to seed. For many this is a very difficult time. Your mentee may begin to pull away from you little by little as she reinvests her seeds in another. She will need time for planting and nurturing seeds in the life of another woman.

To stand by and watch your mentee doing what you know you do well, and freeing that person to succeed—or to make mistakes—takes trusting and letting go.

What a gift of empowering we have in our hands. We must not forget, that gift was placed in our hands by someone else. In a good mentoring relationship, the torch is always passed.

It is much like the old saying: "What goes around comes around." The investment you made with your life will enhance the life of another, and you will be blessed—not once, but over and over. As you watch your mentee grow and mature in the relationship, she will begin blessing others, sharing what she has learned, and you will likewise do the same. Like a wave coming and going with continual motion, the gifts continue to flower and multiply.

Sheldon Vanauken, in *A Severe Mercy*, writes, "Joy is one thing that marked people as true followers of Jesus." Vanauken also says, "Christianity dies a thousand deaths in the life of a joyless Christian." As we abide in Christ, *joy* is God's presence in our life that refreshes others—*joy* is what we should experience when our mentees pull away from us in order to plant their lives in another.

The artwork that my granddaughter, Anna Esther, drew for me is correct. It is because of the overlapping of love from God and our love for God, our joint ownership of the same home, that our heads and hearts are so close. People sense the oneness. The nurture we receive compels us to plant in the soil of another's life, introducing them to the possibility of our connecting relationship with Christ. Almost like identical twins that can't be identified because of their likeness, our oneness overlaps into their mentoring relationship with another. What joy we can experience as our mentees grow and move on!

Mentors transfer the seeds planted in their lives by another—to another. And mentees become mentors.

## The Seeds Multiply and Live On

The heart of a woman on mission will empower other women to see their status is Christ, find entry points to fulfill Christ's purpose in their lives regardless of their spiritual maturity, and reach beyond themselves to touch the world. As a gardener plants seeds, and then divides and multiplies the garden, a woman plants, divides, and multiplies her life when she mentors.

When Melanie Fain came to Samford University, she was a woman of beauty, clothed in the fragrance of Christ. I was privileged to mentor her during her four years as she became a part of my family's life. After graduation she became the secretary in the campus ministry office. This was a wonderful gift to me, since she had worked on the leadership team for four years, led Bible study groups, and, as a student, mentored other students. She came to the position with many gifts. I can remember referring women with prayer concerns to Melanie. She was the fragrance of Christ everywhere she went.

When I left Samford, Melanie was selected to serve as the interim director of Campus Ministries. God used this time to continue to develop her gifts.

I recently spoke at a women's retreat for Melanie's church. It was such a delight to watch the weekend happen and watch her use her leadership and mentoring gifts. She stood beside the women, encouraging, praying for, and guiding the weekend—making a beautiful presentation of fragrance to Christ.

As I stood in the circle to pray with the committee before each session, I could feel the love the leaders had for Melanie and the gratitude that God had let them walk together in the ministry that Melanie leads. We sat late into the night to share all that God was doing in our separate journeys. I was awed by her wise counsel as she walked through a decision with me.

Yes, there you have it! Twenty years ago, I mentored Melanie. Then she mentored me with wise counsel, as the fragrance of Christ from her heart refreshed my own heart and life. Transplanting at its best.

"Everywhere we go, people breathe in the exquisite fragrance. Because of Christ, we give off a sweet scent rising to God, which is recognized by those on the way to salvation." Exquisite fragrance! What a challenge.

Helen Fling has been a role model in my life through the years. From a distance, I observed her love for God and her passion for missions education. *Elegant Lady*—that is the praise I would use in gratitude for her fragrance in my life. Helen wrote the following about those who have mentored her:

> Even one woman who loves God and His world unreservedly has an impact upon other Christian women that is awesome! A chain of influence begins that cannot be terminated, as long as Christ is being lifted up.
>
> As a young pastor's wife in Texas, I was trained and inspired by state WMU leaders, Mrs. R. L. Mathis and Eula Mae Henderson, who created opportunities for service and growth. Later, in conventionwide responsibilities, I was encouraged and mentored by Mrs. Mathis (at that time national president), by Alma Hunt (executive director), and Mrs. William McMurry (staff director). Still later, when I reluctantly succeeded Mrs. Mathis as president, their affirmation was immediate, their help vital.
>
> If limited to naming only one mentor, that one would have to be Mrs. William McMurry. *Mrs. Mac* lived the abundant life among us. Mission study became my magnificent obsession, even as it was hers. She believed that only informed women are inspired women and become influential Christians. However, it was in the area of spiritual growth that she marked our lives profoundly. Indeed, with the exception of my husband and my parents, she contributed more to my spiritual life than any other person.
>
> At this writing, Alma Hunt and I, now well into our eighties, enjoy frequent visits together. We miss our incomparable friends but feel we are *compassed about with so great a cloud of witnesses* as Hebrews 12 suggests. We quote Marie Mathis and Mrs. Mac often, sometimes with tears, sometimes with laughter, but always with longing for younger Christian women to know the excitement and joy of becoming *Laborers Together with God*.
>
> —Helen Fling, president, WMU, SBC (1963–69) and WMU/HMB Promotion Associate in New Areas (1977–84)

I was speaking to a convention of college students from Alabama, Georgia, and Tennessee in the fall of 1995 on the campus of Samford University. After the morning session, I noticed a beautiful young woman waiting at the back of the room. She waited until everyone else finished speaking with me after the service, and then approached me. She introduced herself as Suzanah Raffield, a student at Samford University. She asked if she could walk with me to the gym, where lunch was being served.

As we walked up the hill, she handed me an envelope, telling me it was from a very special friend, Helen Fling. We talked about Helen's influence in each of our lives.

I believe it was the example of Helen that taught me to always carry a handkerchief when I speak. As Suzanah and I parted, I opened the envelope to discover this note and a beautiful hanky from Helen.

October 24, 1995

Esther, m'love,
Indeed, you belong to God and this reality colors your life and ours! In His "loving-kindness and tender mercy," God gave you to your parents, according to His plan, Jeremiah 31:3. And then, joyfully, gave you to Bob . . . to your children . . . to missions and the HMB . . . and now, to your audiences who are profoundly shaped by hearing God speak through you.
Not everyone who hears you, however, has the calling and potential that Suzanah Raffield has, nor the desire to be like you, even to the hanky. I have given her a handkerchief to help her "be like Esther."
I send you a second-hand treasure which belonged first to Marie Mathis and then to me.
Joy! Love!

Your forever friend, Helen F.

I wept. Of course, God is still planting His people. What a reminder from the Father about our responsibility to mentor. Several women in Helen Fling's life spotted the great gifts that God had given her. They stepped in to mentor and encourage

her to develop. Helen, in the winter of her life, has guided me
in the spring and autumn of my life; and she is planting her life
in yet another woman, one who is in the spring of life and just
beginning in God's service. Only the Father knows all that
Suzanah will plant as she lives in obedience to Him.

Do you get it? We are a part of something so much larger
than our realm of existence. How humbling! How exciting! How
challenging! We are women on a mission. It is God's mission,
and He chose to employ us in the ministry of mentoring.

All seasons are open season for mentoring. It does not matter
where you find yourself in the season of your life. It is never
too late to choose to mentor.

*Winter contains spring. Spring gives way to summer. Summer*
*calls for autumn, and autumn rests in winter.*

As one season moves into another season, so does mentoring.
Dig deep into Christ in the winter, nurturing the soil of your
heart, storing up that which you will later share. As the spring of
your life blossoms, divide the plants, sharing your life experiences with others. As summer embraces afternoon showers,
relax and enjoy the beauty of your mentoring relationships. In
autumn, clean the garden bed. Turn the leaves back into the soil
to become nutrients and food for future bulbs and seeds, as the
cycle of mentoring continues. Dig deep into Christ in the winter,
nurturing the soil of your heart, storing up that which you will
later draw on and share. Seeds must die in the garden, so that
they might come to life after winter. It is a clear picture of Christ
dying, so we might live.

In retrospect, in my ten years as the campus minister at Samford University, I mentored and was mentored. My educational
qualifications were slim, but my heart qualifications were strong
and full of love for young people. I had a deep love for missionaries' kids (MKs). Our lives were enriched because so many
MKs chose Samford University as their school.

I don't remember the exact year that Cindy Walker Gaskins
(you'll remember Cindy from Chapter II) and Susan Ingouf
Lafferty, both MKs, came to Samford University, but I will always
remember their individual impact on my life.

Susan's spiritual depth was inspiring. As Susan came on the
campus ministry leadership team, we began to meet on a regular

basis. It was Susan who mentored me in Scripture memorization as we met to pray and share. I came to rely on her spiritual insight, as she embraced our home as her home away from home, and shared our family's love. In my life now, Susan, Todd, and their children hold a place of honor on my prayer wall—that would be the refrigerator—which holds their photo. I intercede for them in their missions field. My heart longs for today's young women to know women who give their lives in missions passion and to know the joy in celebrating God's power as we work together in each other's gardens and labor in His vineyard.

Cindy and Susan, both remarkable women, came into a spring season of my life, and both now serve in the spring of their lives working with women. Susan and her husband, Todd, serve as missionaries in an Eastern country. Cindy and her husband serve in Texas. Cindy's ministry is planting her life into lives of girls in their teen years, and as a pastor's wife, mentoring women of all ages. How humbling to have had the joy of mentoring two such gifted women, and to celebrate God's empowerment in their lives as they continue to pass the torch of leadership. *Yes! God, Yes!*

Grace Chavis is one of South Florida's giant women of prayer. She is a dear friend and prayer warrior with me. Grace wrote:

> Around the age of 50, I felt God leading me to be a Titus 2 woman . . . to teach younger women to love their husbands and have a happy home. This I did through teaching seminars.
>
> One young woman, Anne, was a brilliant atheist who accepted Jesus in one of my Bible classes. Ten years later, she asked me if I would disciple her. Anne said we could meet together any time, and where convenient for me. We studied Kay Arthur's precept course on John. Each of us spent five hours studying alone; then, we met to listen to Kay's tape and discuss as long as I could stay away. She forced me to re-think everything I knew about the Gospel of John! That year became a year of dynamic growth for both of us.
>
> Eight years later when I developed cancer, Anne, who was also an excellent nurse, sought me out and became my personal nurse and mentor through the horrors of chemotherapy. For the past three years, I've been in

The fragrance of Christ is released through disbelief . . . cancer . . . career and friendships. Thank you, Grace Chavis— China Roses, *beauty always near,* to you.

remission. She talks to me on her car phone almost every evening on her way home, asking advice on the day's activities and problems, and discussing Bible principles, and how she can activate them in her work. It is a mother-daughter relationship, for which I thank God.

Bettye Baker is called the *Queen of Division Street* by her husband. She works seven days a week with prostitutes and homeless women and children through Mission Arlington, which is a nonprofit organization affiliated with First Baptist Church, Arlington, Texas. Bettye began her work by giving a luncheon because most of the women on the street live in motel rooms and have no way to cook a hot meal.

She made her way to Division Street to invite women to a luncheon. Twelve women agreed to be picked up for the luncheon; but on the luncheon day, only one showed up. Her response was not that of discouragement. She said, "I wasn't worried. God started it. God was in it and He still is. I have to make a difference one woman at a time." The Wednesday before Thanksgiving 1995, there were 32 in attendance!

What a powerful mentor she is in the lives of the women who live on the street. Sounds just like something Jesus would do! She told me she began this ministry after retirement.

"I had never seen it [the needs of Division Street] because I hadn't looked. I was too busy getting to church!" Bettye said. "I didn't realize [prostitution] was real in Arlington."

A retired woman mentoring prostitutes and their children! My heart bursts with joy as the church is being the church, reflecting God's glory. I'm grateful that this woman came into my life. Her lifestyle has been a challenge to me. She faxes me a cartoon and prayer promises every week. She mentors me constantly.

## The Challenge

Where is your garden? Could you plant a garden of summer missionaries by being a houseparent for a summer? Could you give a bouquet of God's love to loveless women on a Division Street in your town by beginning a Bible study? Would you nurture college students in your community by sharing your home and investing in future leaders? Let the roots in your life push up to flower in another's life—regardless of your *age* or *season.*

The following story is found in the book, *Jesus CEO,* by Laurie Beth Jones:

> One young man, set to run in a one hundred meter race in the Special Olympics, had trained for months and months. But when the gun finally sounded and he leaped out in front of the rest, it seems the excitement of the race overcame him. Each foot went in different directions, and the well-meaning athlete came tumbling down right in front of the starting block. The other racers, each as eager as he was to compete in this great event, nevertheless stopped running their own race and turned back to help him. The crowd came to their feet as his competitors lovingly lifted him up and then walked arm in arm across the finish line together.
>
> These runners in the Special Olympics made me think of Jesus and his set of rules. I thought about him choosing to tell the story about the shepherd who cannot rest as long as even one sheep is still missing, despite the ninety-nine of them which aren't . . . about a father who is waiting on the road, watching for his lost son to come home, even though he has one son who is serving him ably and well . . . about a king holding a banquet, who will not start serving dinner until every place is filled at the Great Table. . . . And I wonder what this world would be like if we played by that rule: that nobody wins until we all do.[1]

Mentors can certainly turn back in the race of life to help someone else. Mentors know that when they take people with them on the journey, the Kingdom of God wins.

I like the idea that mentoring is planting your life in such a way that the impression is lasting and the fragrance impacts the Kingdom of God.

My best friend, Jo Vaughn, is an avid gardener, and she says, "Gardens teach us to share. Some plants grow best when divided and shared, such as the iris"—so does friendship and mentoring.

We are working in a field that does not belong to us. We are all field hands, working to bring honor to the Father.

In *The Message*, 1 Corinthians 3:5–9 reads:

> Who do you think Paul is, anyway? Or Apollos, for that
> matter? Servants, both of us—servants who waited on
> you as you gradually learned to entrust your lives to our
> mutual Master. We each carried our servant assignment.
> I planted the seed, Apollos watered the plants, but God
> made you grow. It's not the one who plants or the one
> who waters who is at the center of this process but
> God, who makes things grow. Planting and watering are
> menial servant jobs at minimum wages. What makes
> them worth doing is the God we are serving. You
> happen to be God's field in which we are working.

As mentors in God's garden, let us commit to pray to the Lord of the harvest, not for our own interests, but rather, for a great harvest from the seeds we have planted in His field.

The garden has been prepared. Seeds will be planted. Love will be extended. Life-giving hope will be transplanted by faithful gardening mentors and mentees.

May your garden path lead you to plant your life in the life of another, releasing the fragrance of Christ.

 Bob and I were transplanting some garden shop plants into the garden when the doorbell rang. It was the garden club president presenting us the Garden-of-the-Month sign for January. We were so surprised. The beauty of our yard is enjoyed by others, just like the fragrance of a mentoring life.

I have come to cherish the time in my garden as this book has taken shape. Quiet visits on the garden swing with my precious husband, Bob, who has retyped and spellchecked every word I've written. To you, my love, bouquets and bouquets of devotion (Heliotrope), which cannot compare to the 60 long-stemmed roses you recently sent me for my 60th birthday. Their fragrance and your love are certainly the fragrance of Christ as you tend my garden heart, encouraging me to keep digging, planting, flowering, and sharing the fragrance of Christ.

# Part Five
# A Garden Retreat

# RELEASING THE FRAGRANCE

*Esther Burroughs*                                      *Bob Burroughs*

Make your-self at home in Me, A-bid-ing in My love; Plant-ing your life in an-oth-er, Re-leas-ing the fra-grance of Christ. Re-leas-ing the fra-grance of Christ.

# A Garden Retreat

- Theme: Releasing the Fragrance of Christ
- Theme Song: "Releasing the Fragrance"
- Scripture: 2 Corinthians 2:14–15 (*The Message*)

"In the Messiah, in Christ, God leads us from place to place in one perpetual victory parade. Through us, he brings knowledge of Christ. Everywhere we go, people breathe in the exquisite fragrance. Because of Christ, we give off a sweet scent rising to God, which is recognized by those on the way to salvation."

Preserving flowers makes a thing of beauty. Preserving godly characteristics in the next generation is not only biblical, (Titus 2:3) but it has eternal values. The retreat suggestions that follow are to assist the leader in connecting the women in the church to each other and God, trusting this will begin some lifelong mentoring habits that will truly impact the Kingdom of God in your church and in your community.

## Retreat Schedule

Several weeks before the retreat, ask each woman who will be attending to purchase and read this book. They may also need to purchase the book you choose for spiritual gifts discovery.

## Friday Evening: Garden Party

**7:00**    Welcome and Special Surprises: Have the room decorated in a garden party theme, with banners, garden tools, seed packages, and plants scattered around the room. Be creative!

Introduce the Scripture theme in a creative way and teach the group the song, "Releasing the Fragrance" which is included in this chapter. It may be reproduced as a part of the retreat.

Knowing the Seeds—Activity #1: Invite the group to number off one through five to form small groups. All the ones get together, all the twos get together, etc.

1. Each group appoints a leader.
2. The group leader asks each person in the group to name their favorite flower and tell why.
3. Provide each group a flip chart and markers. Select an artist-type from your group to draw everyone's favorite flower—or let each person draw her own.

4. Upon completion of the *flower mural,* ask the group to share among themselves funny stories about flowers received or given, or funny garden stories.

5. Ask each group to present their *flower art* to the entire group.

(Note: If this is a large retreat, divide the groups the same way. Let them share their stories in the same way. However, instead of trying to draw a flower for each person in the group, the group can vote on a group favorite. One person from the group will draw it during the large group time on a large mural at the front of the room—making one large flower garden artwork!)

**7:30** Talking About Seeds: Briefly discuss some of the seeds that mentors plant. (See Chapters IV and VI.) Ask the women to think about seeds that might have been planted and nurtured in their lives by another woman. Then ask them to participate in the following activity.

**7:35** Activity #2: Getting Acquainted
1. Invite the women to form two circles with an equal number of people in each group. One circle should form around the other circle—a circle within a circle. The people in the inner circle will be close together, and the people in the outer circle may have to stretch a little, but it will work.
2. When the confusion ends, ask the outer circle to turn left and walk clockwise. Invite the inner circle to turn right and walk counter-clockwise. Each person will place their hands on the shoulders of the person in front of them. Tell them when the music plays (piano or cassette tape), they should begin walking. When the music stops, the circles face each other. Each person then introduces herself to the person in front of her, and tells her about one seed (gift, talent, character trait, etc.) that was planted and nurtured in her by another woman. Those two people are now partners for the rest of this game.
3. Resume game—tell the women that the next time the music stops, they must find their partners and listen for directions. When the music stops, the leader names two body parts, such as knee to elbow, and each must find their partner and place knee to elbow. The last couple to do this is eliminated!
4. Continue this process until only one couple is left. Award daisies—real or fabric—as prizes!

**7:50** Break Time

**8:00** Activity #3
1. Ask each person to take the notepaper provided and list their role models or mentors. Instruct them to leave space between each name. Allow two minutes.
2. Direct women to return to the top of their list and next to each person's name, write a word to describe that person. Ask them to jot down a bit of wisdom they found in one of the times they shared tears or laughter with this person.
3. Say, "If each of these people could be here at this time, what do you think they would say to us as a group?" Allow time for reflection. Ask the women to share their responses with their partners from the previous activity. Then ask several people to share their responses with the whole group.
4. Close this session by reading the story about Marge Caldwell (Chapter I, pp. 4–5). Invite the group to act upon their memories and if possible, when they return home, write and thank the persons they listed.

**8:30** Activity #4: Invite each participant to take whichever gift inventory you have selected (see p. 122 for suggestions) to their room and complete it before turning in for the night. Instruct roommates to discuss the results—or following directions found in the gifts book you have selected, incorporate a more detailed discussion of spiritual gifts into your time on Saturday. Good night to all!

**Saturday Morning**
**7:00** Breakfast: At breakfast, place collage paper at the back of the eating area on tables—one for each group. Invite the groups from the previous night to find the collage paper and think of one mentor, role model, or parent. Ask them to write those names on the collage and write one word or a sentence that describes this person.

**7:45** Read John 15:1–17 (from *The Message*, if possible). Ask the group to join in singing "Releasing the Fragrance." Have a time of singing praise songs and sharing testimony. Enlist someone to sing "Show Yourselves to Be," by Steven Curtis Chapman.

**8:00**　　Invite the group to discuss the following questions with a friend. The friend may be new or old, but preferably someone different from the roommate they discussed their gifts with the ꞏ night before. It is important to receive the affirmation of our spiritual gifts from Christian friends. Ask each other these questions: 1) What did the test say my gifts are? 2) What gifts do you see in me? 3) What gifts do I see in myself? 4) How could this gift be used to mentor someone?

After this dialogue, invite each person to write their gift on the collage and sign their name. Read aloud a few of the listed gifts—these are enough, certainly, to make an impact in the Kingdom of God.

**8:25**　　Ask the women to sit with their partners and spend some time in prayer, thanking God for the gifts and asking for wisdom to use these gifts to mentor someone else.

**8:30**　　Now ask each person to choose another woman from their group to be a new partner. Discuss: On a scale of one to ten (ten being the highest), What is *my abiding-in-Christ* level? What things in my life do I trust more than my relationship to Christ? *Allow ten minutes.*

Reference the Roger and Diane McMurrin story in Chapter VII, page 58 of the book, then pose these questions:
• What are you presently doing in your life that will remain when you are gone?
• Share your abiding or quiet time habits.

Instruct the group to:
• Make three columns across a page, and place the words *friendship, parenting,* and *mentoring* at the top of the columns.
• Define each of these three areas using one word. Make a list of one-word definitions under each word. Discuss differences and similarities.

**9:15**　　Break

**9:30**　　Instruct the group to get into groups of four. Share the story of Cindy Landry in Chapter III, pages 22–23, and lead into the activity of sharing books with each other. (Those attending the retreat should have been asked to bring their favorite book.)

**9:50** Give each person a chance to share what the book meant in her life, as time allows. Give them an opportunity to exchange books. Be sure the *name, address, and phone number* are in each book, so books can be returned!

**10:15** In the same groups of four, invite the women to share life verses and tell the story of what God has taught them through the Scripture. Show each other your Bibles and the marked verses from your life journeys. Ask the women to share from the devotional books and helps they use. Invite one or two from small groups to share a Scripture promise journey with the group.

Tell this story: The florist prepared the basket of flowers. A woman watched him take a closed iris bud and begin tapping it with his thumb and middle finger. She was amazed as the iris opened to be placed in the arrangement. He explained, "That's how you wake up a flower—just a gentle tap." Some mentees need a gentle tap to begin reading God's Word for life promises and instructions.

**10:45** Transplanting: Invite the women to get in groups of three for this exercise.

If mentoring is a partnership between two persons for the purpose of mutual growth, suggest the women make a gardening/mentoring list, like a master gardener makes a monthly gardening list. Mentoring takes time and planning. It doesn't just happen. Ask the groups to write their lists, like the sample below. You'll duplicate these lists later and distribute them at the next women's meeting or through Sunday School classes. These are transplanting ideas that will enrich everyone.

Example:
*January:* Plan a churchwide event, such as a dessert party for mentors/mentees. Make plans to begin meeting twice a month, and plan a phone call twice a month to begin getting acquainted.
*February:* Go to lunch together for the fun of it. Meet once this month as you begin a Bible/book study together. Set goals to finish the study individually and then share together.

**11:30** Break until lunch at 12:00 noon.

## Saturday Afternoon

**1:00**    Make a poster of this quote. "Every no makes room for a yes. Every yes crowds out a no. Every yes and no needs balance."

Invite the group to read pages 79–83 of Chapter X before beginning the next activity. Allow ten minutes for this activity, done individually.

Ask, When you remember that you can be only one place at a time, what do you need to take from your *yes* list and put on your *no* list? Or do you need to change a *no* to a *yes*?

**1:30**    Invite the group to look at the advice for mentors and mentees on pages 10–12 in Chapter I. After they have read these pages, instruct the group to answer the questions in their notebook. Share the Helen Fling story on pages 105–108 of Chapter XIII. Invite women to get into dyads. Invite them to draw a gift box in their notebooks the size of half a page.

Ask, What kind of things would you like to put in your gift box, things that make you feel delight, i.e., a card, a visit, Scripture promise. Write these words in your gift box. Share with each other. Invite several from the group to share what they said with the entire group.

Point out how rewarding it is to mentor and share friendship. Invite them to follow up on this in the next two months, doing one of the things their partner said made her feel delight.

**2:00**    For the closing session of the retreat, invite several women (in advance) to read or tell selected stories from the books—stories that inspired them.

This should empower them to prayerfully consider what happens in God's field when they choose to mentor by planting in the life of another.

Sing the theme song as a closing prayer.

# Endnotes

## Part One: Principles of Garden Design

Chapter I: This Is It!
[1]Susan Hunt, *Spiritual Mothering* (Wheaton, IL: Good News Publishers/Crossway Books, 1992), 27. Used by permission.

Chapter III: Plotting the Possibilities
[1]James Underwood Crockett, *Crockett's Flower Garden* (Boston/Toronto: Little, Brown and Company, 1981), 30.

## Part Two: Cultivating and Sowing

Chapter V: Working the Soil
[1]Frances Hodgson Burnett, *The Secret Garden* (New Jersey: dilithium Press, Ltd., 1987).

Chapter VI: Sowing the Seeds
[1]Recorded on the album, *For the Sake of the Call,* Word Records.
[2]To order the *Do Unto Others Plate,* contact the Golden Rule Plate Company, Inc., P. O. Box 26404, Little Rock, AR 72221; (501) 227-9930.

## Part Three: Nurturing Growth

Chapter XI: Supplying Support
[1]Used by permission from *Journey* © 1996 LifeWay Press.

## Part Four: Releasing the Fragrance

Chapter XIII: Garden Dividends
[1]Laurie Beth Jones, *Jesus CEO* (New York: Hyperion). Used by permission.

*Part Five: A Garden Retreat*

Books That Contain Spiritual Gifts Tests:

Barbara Joiner, *Yours for the Giving: Spiritual Gifts* (Birmingham, AL: Woman's Missionary Union, 1986).
R. Wayne Jones, *Using Spiritual Gifts: How to Discover and Use Spiritual Gifts* (Nashville, TN: Broadman Press, 1985).
Tim Blanchard, *A Practical Guide to Finding Your Spiritual Gifts* (Wheaton, IL: Tyndale House Publishers, Inc., 1979).

For More Information on Spiritual Gifts:

Kenneth S. Hemphill, *Spiritual Gifts: Empowering the New Testament Church* (Nashville, TN: Broadman Press, 1988).
Larry Gilbert, *Team Ministry: A Guide to Spiritual Gifts and Lay Involvement* (Lynchburg, VA: Church Growth Institute, 1987).